When the Honeymoon's Over

When the Honeymoon's Over:

Making the Most of Your First Year of Marriage

DAVID AND VERA MACE

Abingdon Press / Nashville

WHEN THE HONEYMOON'S OVER

This book is printed on acid-free paper.

Library of Congress Cataloging-in-Publication Data

Mace. D. R. (David Robert
  When the honeymoon's over : making the most of your first year of
marriage / David and Vera Mace.
  marrip. cm.
  Bibliography: p.
  ISBN 0-687-45040-3 (pbk. : alk. paper)
  1. Marriage—United States. 2 Communication in marriage—United
States. 3. Interpersonal relations. 4. Marriage counseling—United
States. I. Mace, Vera. II. Title.
HQ734.M18448 1988   88-22230
646.7'8—dc 19   CIP

MANUFACTURED BY THE PARTHENON PRESS AT
NASHVILLE, TENNESSEE, UNITED STATES OF AMERICA

To Martha Jane Starr,
whose concern and support made possible
both the writing of this book
and the program it describes

CONTENTS

PREFACE

This book is written, first and foremost, for couples very recently, or soon to be, married—either for the first time or remarrying.

We believe we have an important and encouraging message for you. But you are also faced today with some very discouraging facts—mainly the prediction that many of you may fail in marriage and end up getting divorced.

This is a disturbing prospect, we agree. But we are now deeply convinced that this state of affairs *need not continue*. It is the result of a situation that, in the light of the knowledge we now have, can be changed.

Modern marriage has become like a stretch of highway on which many tragic accidents happen because the road needs a number of repairs. We now have the power, if we are ready to face the situation seriously, to make those repairs and to end up with a much better road than ever before.

Without going into a lot of detail, let us try to summarize the situation.

1. Marriages generally are no less happy than they were before. Our *expectations* of marriage, however, are much higher today. If these are not realized, divorce offers a way out that is now acceptable in our society.

2. Marriage in the past was a one-vote system. The husband was boss, and the wife had no alternative but to be obedient and responsive to his wishes. Now this has changed, and we have a two-vote system, which is much better, but is also much more difficult to manage.

3. In the past, marriage was the only acceptable way to have a readily available sex partner. The sexual revolution, as it is called, has changed all that; however the threat of AIDS is now bringing the new freedom to a screeching halt.

4. The new status of women offers the option for modern marriage to be an equal partnership. This is good, but it makes adjustment to marriage much more difficult than it has been before.

5. While the new companionship marriage is far more deeply satisfying than the old system, achieving it requires much knowledge and skill that was never needed in the past.

These profound changes in the marriage system just aren't clearly understood by most people today. But the behavioral sciences have been bringing us vital new knowledge, and we now have the answers to most of our questions. Today we know just what it takes to make marriages much happier than they have ever been. The result of this situation is that at the very time that so many marriages are failing, those that are succeeding are better and happier than ever before.

Unfortunately, this information has not been communicated to most of the people marrying today. So, while we have the answers, it must be clearly understood that a really satisfying modern marriage is the result of skills that have to be learned and practiced. This takes as much work and planning as success in a high-level career. We can now show couples how to succeed, but only if they are prepared to learn how to work hard at it. The choice is up to you.

In this book, we have tried to put together some of the new knowledge we have and to describe some of the new skills you will need in order to achieve the "companionship marriage," as we call it. However, *reading the book will not be enough.* What it will do is tell you *how to learn the new skills* you will need. The rest is up to you. All we are saying is that answers are available, but you will have to do the work of applying them!

We have written this book primarily for newlyweds, because we think you will be interested in it, and we believe that you will find it helpful. However, we hope that as we talk to you, a few other people will be looking over your shoulders and listening to what we have to say. What kinds of people? Marriage specialists in the various disciplines; ministers and rabbis who marry couples; and above all, influential persons who have the power to influence communities to provide newlywed programs like the ones we describe and advocate.

CONTRIBUTORS TO THIS BOOK

Though we, David and Vera Mace, actually wrote this book, we didn't do it alone. We had substantial aid from a team of helpers, all well qualified and certified leaders in the Association for Couples in Marriage Enrichment (ACME) and all having been involved in programs that have already helped hundreds of newly-wed couples in different parts of the country. They include specialists in the fields of psychology, medicine, religion, and social work. They are listed here and are described in *Appendix 1*.

Our ACME custom, when introducing married couples, is to treat them as equals, listing their names in alphabetical order and without titles or university degrees. Here they are, with their locations.

Alvis and Florence Carpenter, Clemmons, North Carolina
Lyle and Terry Dykstra, Baltimore, Maryland
Bill and Linda McConahey, South Boston, Virginia
Phyllis and Randy Michael, Kansas City, Kansas
Alice and Richard Robertson, Columbus, Georgia
Doris and Jerry Thompson, Nashville, Tennessee

We wish also to pay tribute to Martha Jane Starr of Kansas City, without whose initiative and support these programs for newlyweds might never have developed; to Alice and Hampton Morgan, who launched the program in Winston-Salem, North Carolina, whose program was later taken over by the Carpenters; and to Joan and Keith Hackett of Vancouver, Washington, who are now beginning a program in their home community. Again, all are members of the ACME organization.

We would like also to express our gratitude to Eleanor Eklund.

What Newlyweds
Need to Know

1

Marriage Building Is a Tough Task

In this book, we talk with you about an important area of your lives. You are moving, or have recently moved, into marriage and, naturally, you want your marriage to be a success. Just what you are expecting you know better than we do. But we have a pretty good idea, because we are also a married couple, and we have spent most of the years of our shared life working on our own relationship and helping other married couples to find happiness together. After all this time, we know pretty well what most couples need in order to succeed, and we want to share that knowledge with you.

The average couple of today have almost no idea about how much is now known about marriage. For a good part of this century, experts have been studying close relationships. With their help, we now have put together a great deal of valuable knowledge that could make all the difference to you as a newly married couple. This valuable information is stored in hundreds of books, but most couples just don't have time to spend hours in libraries or to take courses or to attend lectures. So we have a state of affairs in which the couples who need the knowledge can't get it. They often grope blindly in their attempts to cope with complicated situations that are making them miserable. The answers are there, but somehow people don't know how to find them or how to use them.

MARRIAGE BUILDING IS A TOUGH TASK

It isn't really as simple as that. Even if you do find the right book to explain the problem you are struggling with, all you get is an *intellectual* answer, and that just isn't enough. Coping with the many problems of modern marriage can be a complicated task, as we know very well from our own personal experience. What you really need is not just an *explanation* of what is happening to you. Above all, you want to see another couple like yourselves *actually dealing* with the problem you can't seem to solve. Then you can identify with Jane and Peter, watch how they tackle the situation, and apply this to what you see happening in your own relationship. Can this be arranged? Yes, indeed, it can. We are actually doing it now, though so far on a limited scale. But the prospects for the future are exciting. Let us try to tell the story briefly, so that you can understand the possibilities we are now able to offer you.

All over the world, for thousands of years, couples have been getting married. Each continent, each country, each island, and each tribe has had its own customs, which have been passed on from one generation to the next. These customs have been studied and described by scholars in big books. We now have a great deal of information about the history of marriage.

The man who first tried to put it all together was Edward Westermarck, a university professor in Finland, who later also became a professor at London University in England. His book, *The History of Human Marriage*, first published in 1890, a hundred years ago, told of marriage customs all over the world. He kept collecting more information, and by the year 1920 he had three big volumes with more than five hundred pages in each.

Other writers began to join in, and hundreds of books about marriage have now been published in many languages. At first most of them were technical books for students to read, but in time popular books began to appear, written for ordinary couples to try to answer some of the questions they were asking. You have probably seen some of these books, and you may have read one or two of them

Why do we have marriage at all? This is an important question, and it isn't difficult to answer. Every couple getting married have a right to ask the question, and they deserve a clear answer.

All our human marriage systems have existed for three purposes. Sometimes one purpose has seemed more important than the others, and over time the emphasis has shifted. But you need to understand all three to get the full picture.

The first and most important purpose is *the passing on of human life from one generation to the next*. All living things eventually die. We have ancient trees in California that were alive in the time of Christ, but they will eventually die. On the other hand, some insects live only a few days, and are quickly replaced by others. At the human level, a few people live for as long as a hundred years, but in the end others take their places, generation by generation. So the main purpose of marriage is to produce, to protect, to support, to guide, and to train the children who will become the citizens of the future, carrying on the traditions of our culture. Marriage provides the foundation for the family, and it is through family life that our culture is passed on from generation to generation. That is absolutely fundamental.

This leads us naturally to the second purpose of marriage, which is *to meet our sexual needs*. In the animal world, to which we also belong, sex is the means by which life is continued over time. Some very simple living cells just split in half—one into two—and that is enough. But more complex creatures need the system of two uniting to produce one new life. The sex drive gets this done, and it has to be a very strong drive to make sure that life really is continued.

Human sexuality is, likewise, a very strong drive. However, while many newborn animals can take care of themselves soon after birth, human beings are much more complex and need years to grow to maturity. During those years, they have to be fed and cared for, educated and trained, before they reach adulthood and, at the age of twenty-one in our culture, become full citizens and take over the culture as it moves into the new generation.

Obviously, a strong and enduring link is necessary to bind together the father and mother and the parents and their children, in this long-term partnership. Since people sometimes don't measure up to their full human duties both Church and State have had to join together to see that the vital task of parenthood is properly carried out and to prevent people from just enjoying the sexual experience and walking away from their responsibilities. That is what is beginning to happen often in our communities today; the State has made divorce easy, and as a result families are breaking up in increasing numbers.

This has led to a crisis in our culture. To meet this crisis, we shall have to depend on the third purpose of marriage: *the companionship relationship between the partners*. This has often seemed unimportant in the past. Wives generally have had many children, and this has kept them at home on a full-time basis while their husbands went out to work in the wider world. Since motherhood consumed their time and energy, there seemed to be no need for wives to be involved, as their husbands were, in higher levels of education or to learn the skills needed for a career in a profession or business. So the concept of marriage was not of an equal companionship, but rather of a dominant husband involved in the outside world and of an obedient wife occupied with the care of home and children.

The change that is now in progress has made husband and wife equal, and in many cases they are both now involved in the outside world. The result, inevitably, is that marriage has changed its nature and has become a companionship between equal partners. This is not an easy situation to deal with, because we have never before had to view both marriage partners as fully equal in their involvement outside the home, so that neither of them is able to take sole responsibility for child rearing.

The results of this changing pattern are plain to see. The task of parenting is often making apparently unreasonable demands on the working parents. Some husbands are abandoning their responsibilities and walking out on their marriages. These absentee fathers are now able to find other women who will have sex with them, without requiring anything in return.

Meanwhile, the deserted wives lack both the time and the money to function effectively as parents. As a result, children are being born in numbers too small to maintain the population; many of those who *are* being born lack the support and training they need to develop into mature and responsible adults. Meanwhile, the traditional controls on sex are collapsing, and even young adolescent boys find themselves free to have casual relations with girls, without having to assume any responsibility for children who may be born as a result.

As an inevitable consequence of these changes, the

importance of the marriage system for the preservation of our culture seems to have been forgotten. The Protestant churches, at the time of the Reformation, handed over to the State the responsibility of supervising marriage, but now the collapse of nearly all the controls, making divorce easily available, is threatening to destroy our whole family system. One result is that, on an increasing scale, some couples who are attracted to each other just don't bother to get married, but simply live together, without producing children, until they grow tired of each other and go their separate ways.

All these events, which have happened in the course of this century, have thrown our society into a state of great confusion. Some people think we can manage all right by giving up our marriage and family system altogether and by arranging for children to be raised by the State. This would mean a dramatic change and the abandonment of the parenthood concept that has been basic to the whole history of human culture. Besides, marriage itself has played a vital part in teaching responsibility to men and women and has been a cause of great happiness to many couples.

Before we take the awesome risk of giving up our marriage system, therefore, we ought to make a real effort to understand what is happening and to find out how to adapt the system to some of the changes in the culture. In order to do this, some of us who have found deep and lasting fulfillment in the experiences of marriage and parenthood now feel that we must speak out to the new generation and help them to develop the new "companionship marriage" that means so much to us and that we see as the hope of the future.

2

Understanding Romantic Love and Real Love

Every modern marriage that is legally recognized must begin with a ceremony. We call it a wedding, from the verb *to wed*, which means that the two partners are joined together in a shared life. The word *wedlock* makes it clear that this is intended to be a lasting attachment. The couple are locked together—for life; at least, that was the original intention.

In former times, the life span was much shorter than it is today. The expectation was to have plenty of children, who had to be raised to adulthood. If the parents lived long enough to need to be cared for, it was the duty of the grown-up children to provide this care. Usually all of them lived their lives in the same community, and they eventually died there.

Often the parents chose the marriage partners for their children. We can remember being present at a Muslim wedding in Pakistan in which the partners were both young teenagers. They had been brought together by both sets of parents and had never met each other before the wedding. Only when the ceremony was over was the bridegroom allowed to lift the veil and see, for the first time, the face of his wife.

The system of parents choosing marriage partners for their children has been quite common throughout the world. The idea of romantic love as the basis for marriage is a relatively modern concept. In the Middle Ages, romantic love was celebrated widely in poems and songs, but it was seldom associated with marriage, which was by contrast a severely practical, down to earth arrangement between families.

In our time, however, marriage is seen as being almost entirely based on romance. A couple feel the drawing power of a strong attraction to each other, and they take this to mean that they are suited to embark together on a shared life. Being "in love" is simply accepted as the necessary evidence that they will be able to adapt to each other. Plato, the Greek philosopher, spoke about a belief that men and women were originally joined to each other in pairs. Then the gods, in a mischievous mood, tore them apart and scattered them. What each then had to do was to search diligently for his or her lost other half and then be reunited!

Romantic fantasies are a pleasant part of our day-to-day life, and should be recognized as such. Love is certainly the foundation stone of a happy and enduring marriage. But we need to be realistic about choosing and relating to our marriage partners. So let us be severely practical about what being "in love" really means.

We have seen that sexual attraction is a dynamic force that brings a man and a woman together. It has to be a very powerful force because it is the sexual mating of male and female that sustains life, since death comes sooner or later. Only if we have produced offspring can there be any future for the species to which we belong. As we all know, living creatures—the dinosaurs, for example—once inhabited the earth, but have now died out. We say that they are now "extinct."

So the sex drive has to be very powerful. If a male

animal becomes aware that a female is present and that she is ready to be impregnated, he will abandon anything else he was planning to do and go after her. If in so doing he finds another male animal who is also going after her, the two males may fight each other furiously to gain exclusive possession of the female.

At most animal levels, however, once the male has sexually impregnated the female, he can walk away and forget all about it. When, later, the young offspring are born, the mother is entirely capable of taking care of their needs for the short time before they are sufficiently developed to become independent.

We may not like having our behavior associated with that of animals, but we just can't understand what is happening to us otherwise. The fact must be faced that slipping back to the animal level is something that can easily happen. For example, the easy availability of many women today for casual sexual experiences is causing numbers of men to take what they can get and then walk away, with no regard for the possible obligations of fatherhood.

It is necessary, therefore, for us to examine carefully what we are talking about in reference to marriage when we use the word *love*, which can have at least two very different meanings.

What we call "romantic love" is based on sexual attraction. A man meets a woman whom he finds physically attractive, and he begins to be sexually aroused. This is all perfectly natural. At the animal level, he is aware of a strong desire to have intercourse with her. But, of course, he doesn't say this, either to her or to himself. What he sees in her is a fine, attractive image of womanhood at its best. As such, she obviously appears to him as someone he might like to marry, because she would then be a readily available sex partner. However, if she also has admirable personal qualities, this adds to her attractiveness, so the sexual interest can conveniently be kept in the background.

Next, he begins a friendship with this woman. They find they have many interests in common, just as might be the case with a good friend of their own sex. Over time, the relationship develops between them. The woman is at the same time going through a similar process, a combination of sexual attraction and interpersonal friendliness. Then, if the relationship continues to develop at both levels, they begin to talk about marriage as a possibility.

We define the condition of this man and woman by saying that they are "in love" with each other. What we mean is that they are powerfully attracted to each other sexually and also have a number of shared viewpoints and common interests. This is regarded as the right and proper basis for a possible marriage.

Freud described romantic love as "aim-inhibited sex." This recognized the fact that, at least in the culture of that time, the factor of sexual desire, which was drawing two people to each other, couldn't be openly acknowledged; it was described as a feeling of love for each other as persons. Of course, it is possible to love another person—a child or a parent or a colleague—without any sexual factor being involved. Indeed, a sexual factor in such a relationship would be entirely inappropriate. So love as an emotional state has two quite separate meanings. You can love a person for his or her worth, regardless of gender; you can love a person who is sexually attractive; and you can love a person at both of these levels.

We have, perhaps, labored this distinction between

the two different kinds of love, which are both vitally necessary for a successful companionship marriage. It might, in fact, be wise to say, by way of having a clear definition, that a really meaningful marriage is a combination of companionship love and sexual love.

If this is clear, we can now take the discussion a stage further. These two kinds of love play quite different roles in marriage. Sexual love normally awakens the couple to a *physical* interest in each other, something different and more compelling than companionship love. At the beginning of the marriage, it is the major factor in holding the couple together. But gradually, over time, its power and influence diminish in a cooling down process. Studies have shown that the frequency of sexual intercourse drops in most marriages during the first year. In a sense, the sexual attraction has served its purpose in bringing the two together into a shared life.

Now, however, the real task of marriage begins: the bringing of two lives into a state of mutual cooperation and harmony, through the sharing of common interests and mutual support. In other words, they must now become *companions* who have teamed up together to pursue common goals in a shared life. If this is not done, the romantic love that brought them together cannot sustain the relationship, and it will gradually die away.

This explains why so many marriages today are failing in the first few years. The dynamic that brought them together is now a spent force. Romantic love is powerful, but may be short-lived; it must be combined with companionship love if the relationship is to grow over time and become meaningful.

What we have come to see very clearly is that the critical time for you as a couple to begin working at your marriage is your first year together. The drive of sexual love unites you and gets you started. However, unless you have already begun the much more complex task of building companionship love together, the dynamic of the relationship falls away and becomes spent. The common attitude that suggests that in the first year of marriage you can rest on your laurels and freely enjoy a rich and rewarding experience is not based on reality. The honeymoon may still represent that glamorous sense of serene fulfillment. But once you are back from the honeymoon, the real work of building a lasting marriage has to begin. Otherwise, there is a distinct possibility of disillusionment and failure.

In the past, it has been considered unnecessary to help couples until they have gotten into serious trouble, when the aim was to reverse the process that had produced disillusionment and conflict. Only now is it becoming clear how unrealistic this is. We will try to explain this preventive approach in some detail in the next chapter.

3

The Best Way to Help Marriages

It may surprise you to know that the whole idea of helping couples to develop a good marriage is relatively new and that we are only now beginning to understand how to do it. It happens that we—David and Vera—have been pioneers in this new field. So the best way we can explain it will be to tell you, briefly, our life story.

We were married in the year 1933, which is quite a long time ago. What we are telling you about the development of the companionship marriage is, in part, the story of our own life together. We were married in London, England. We had read some books about the subject, but they would seem quaint by modern standards. At that time, we were working in a London slum area in the depths of a very serious economic depression. All around us were people suffering from acute poverty, unemployment, and despair; at that time there were very few of the social services that came later with the welfare state. We saw tragedy and crime everywhere. We called it "life with the lid off."

Faced with this widespread misery, we decided, and told our assembled relatives and friends at our wedding, that we wanted to spend our lives working together to make the world a happier place. We have never departed from that decision.

As we considered how to begin this tremendous task, we looked for a starting point. We noticed that a few people, in all the confusion and tragedy, seemed able to cope with life. When we asked them why, they nearly all said that it was because they had been raised in happy families. When we investigated these families, we nearly always found that they were the results of good marriages. So we decided that the quality of human relationships is the key to a better world and that the marriage relationship is the foundation stone on which better human relationships can best be built. If this sounds rather simplistic, we admit that we are still of the same opinion.

Our motto is: Work for better marriages, beginning with our own. We still hold to that purpose. It is the reason we have written this book.

We began by reading everything we could find about marriage. You guessed right—there wasn't much! We searched for organizations that helped couples with their marriages. At that time there were none at all. The whole subject was avoided and seldom even talked about.

We then met a Presbyterian minister, Dr. Herbert Gray, who had an idea. He wanted to start a new British organization and to call it the Marriage Guidance Council. He had a few supporters, most of them physicians, who were at that time the only people to whom married couples could talk about their problems. The organization was established, and members started giving public lectures about marriage—something that had never been done before.

Then came World War II, which caused the widespread breakup of family life in Britain. We opened a Marriage Guidance Center in London, near the American Embassy. We were at once swamped by people needing help, and we had to seek supporters. The idea caught on, and seven years later the National Marriage Guidance Council, as we called it, had a hundred centers established all over Britain. Our work was recognized and supported by the British Government and has been ever since.

Dealing with these troubled couples taught us a great deal about marriage. In the following years we were invited to go to other countries to help start similar services and to train counselors to staff them.

Meanwhile, we moved to the United States and settled here. In New York City, the American Association of Marriage Counselors had already set up a national headquarters and had opened an office. However, it didn't get enough support at first, and the office had to be closed. At that critical point, we were asked if we would be willing to take it over. At first we were hesitant to undertake such a task, but in the end we did so. In another seven years we had developed what has now become the American Association for Marriage and Family Therapy, with over ten thousand clinical members all over the country.

As you know, marriage counseling is now widely recognized in most of the developed countries, and we are glad we had a share in getting it started. However, in time we began to have some further ideas. In our counseling, we had always recorded "case histories." We kept discovering that the problems couples brought for help had usually been developing for a long time and were often difficult to clear up after years of conflict. We began to realize that most of the services now available to help marriages succeed are confined to what we call the "before and after" areas.

We had been trying to offer couples marriage prepa-

ration, which is largely undertaken b
the couples they will later marry. W
until some couples began to get in'
we offered them marriage *coun*
wonder whether it would be possible ᴜ
earlier stage in the marriage and work *preventiveⅼy*
couples.

It wasn't until 1962 that we were able to try out this new idea. We led weekend retreats for small groups of married couples—not couples with serious problems this time, but just couples who would like to *improve* their marriages. As we worked with them, we found that some of them already had symptoms that might lead to serious trouble later. We also found, however, that with a little help from us and from other couples in the group who had faced similar situations, they could clear up their difficulties and avoid later problems.

In other words, we had found a way to catch possible serious problems early and prevent them from developing any further. As we led more and more of these weekend retreats, we became convinced that we had discovered something very important.

At that point we also saw that, although marital therapy would always continue to be necessary for some couples, we must combine with it the kinds of preventive services that we had now discovered and that were proving, on the small scale on which we were offering them, to be highly effective. To describe what we were doing, we decided to use the term *marriage enrichment*, which is now widely used. While we had been first in the field in the United States, we found that a somewhat similar movement, called Marriage Encounter, had been started by the Roman Catholic Church in Spain, also in the year 1962, which was brought to this country in 1967.

, were opening for the offering to married couples
ntirely new kinds of *preventive* services, though the
already developed remedial services would, of course,
still be necessary.

While we were continuing to experiment with
marriage enrichment, we moved to Winston-Salem,
North Carolina, where David became a professor in the
Bowman Gray Medical School. Here we were able to lead
many marriage enrichment retreats. As more and more
local couples became involved, we decided, on our
fortieth wedding anniversary, to start a new national
organization: the Association for Couples in Marriage
Enrichment, ACME for short. This Association has
spread in time across the United States and Canada and
has now become international.

At this point, we began to train carefully selected
married couples to lead ACME retreats. We set high
standards. No individual leadership was involved,
because we were convinced that couple leadership
represented the best approach. We considered it
desirable that at least one member of the leader couple
should have had experience of interviewing other people
about how to deal with personal or interpersonal
problems, though we have allowed occasional exceptions to that rule. The couple had to have been involved
in at least one marriage enrichment event, with a
favorable report from the leader couple of that event,
before being accepted for training. They then had to go
through "basic training," after which they must lead two
retreats, with favorable reports from the participants;
then the leader couple could take part in an advanced
training workshop. This system has all worked out well,
and our certified couples, now worldwide, have given

and continue to give excellent service. Marriage enrichment is still new and is not yet widely known, but it is now becoming more and more recognized.

One more development has taken place, and that concerns the subject of this book. Once we had become involved in the preventive approach, we saw the obvious wisdom of involving the entire marriage from its beginning. We were *not* offering help to newlyweds in their first year or two together. Somehow this was considered unnecessary and even inappropriate. It is all part of what we call the "intermarital taboo."

One day we came across a report of a study of divorced couples that had been undertaken in England. The couples were of all ages, and they had been invited to describe their experiences. The study reported that no less than one-third of them admitted that *they had already been in serious trouble by the time they reached their first wedding anniversary!*

This was a challenge that we couldn't evade. We knew that the view of most people was that the first year of marriage is a serene and happy time—a kind of extension of the honeymoon, when the beginnings of the shared life bring great joy and no problems. Yet here was evidence that this is not always so.

We decided to take action. That was in the year 1979, and at the time ACME was developing a major marriage enrichment program in Kansas City, Missouri. We decided that this offered us an opportunity to try out an experimental program for newlyweds. A plan was worked out. Some certified ACME leader couples were available, and we decided to give them additional training and then use them to lead special events for newlywed couples.

This program at first covered four evenings at weekly intervals, but it soon had to be extended to six evenings. The success of this project has now led to its being introduced in four other American communities. We shall come back to this, and give you a detailed report of it, later.

4

After the Honeymoon, What?

Our culture cherishes a rosy picture of the first year of marriage. The first year is supposed to be a serenely happy experience, with the couple deeply fulfilled after the difficult process of finding each other, making up their minds about whether this is the right choice, making all kinds of decisions, and planning ahead. Now all the uncertainties are cleared up, and the couple are starting out on a well-worn road that should lead to a happy future.

This rosy picture begins with the honeymoon—a relaxed period, usually spent in a location that offers beauty and peace. The new husband and wife are expected to enjoy an uninterrupted period of great pleasure and undisturbed relaxation.

The period following the honeymoon hardly continues that experience. It is seen as a pleasant time of "settling down" in a new home and beginning a shared life in which the earlier experience of single loneliness is over. The couple can enjoy their mutual love and give each other mutual support.

Because this is seen as a time when the couple enjoy the fulfillment of their hopes and dreams, there is generally an understood agreement on the part of their family and friends that the couple should be left alone as much as possible. Certainly it would seem poor judgment for us to ask them whether they are having difficulties or needing help. So, if we feel the need to give information, guidance, or support, this seems not to be the time to do it.

Acting on this assumption, we have organized our services to marriage in a clearly defined pattern. First, we offer "marriage preparation." As the Boy Scouts keep reminding us, it is always wise to "be prepared" for what lies ahead. So we have "premarital counseling"; within reasonable limits that can be a good idea. But we need to point out that, in principle, this is rather like teaching people to swim by explaining the strokes with drawings on the chalkboard. We must remember that it is when people get into the water that the real learning process takes place!

Following the wedding, couples are generally left alone, to sink or to swim. If, however, they really show signs of sinking, which they almost dare not do as early as the first year, they must struggle on as best they can, with any call for help viewed as inappropriate or irresponsible.

After the first year or two, however, it becomes all right to ask for help. At that point we have now marshaled all kinds of services to which they can turn. These are available from physicians, psychologists, social workers, pastors, and marital therapists who are specialists in the field.

This is the system we have established. The message this system seems to send to couples is that it is inappropriate for them to need help in their first year together, because at that stage the occurrence of "problems" implies that they are somewhat incompetent, or even irresponsible, in developing trouble so soon after their wedding. The implication is clear. What we are saying in effect is: "Don't bother us with your *little* difficulties. You should be able to deal with them by yourselves. Come to us only when you are in *real* trouble and when you have exhausted all your own resources in the attempt to clear it up."

Another restraining factor is that if you want a really competent counselor to help you, there is a price to pay. Highly skilled marital therapists have had to get extensive and costly training, and they are, therefore, entitled to be paid at appropriate rates. Consequently, couples may tend to struggle on alone as long as they can. By the time paying the cost of skilled help seems the only hope for them, they may be inclined to take the apparently easier alternative of divorce.

We have tried to give you a fair and accurate account of the situation that confronts the recently married couple in, and soon after, their first year together. Now we want to offer a somewhat different picture of what might be done and what we are proposing as an alternative.

We will go back to that study, made in England, that found that one in three of the married couples who were ultimately divorced admitted to having been in serious trouble on their first anniversary. We are not concerned to ask whether that can be taken as an accurate estimate. What we are concerned about is that we want *no* married couples to find themselves in serious trouble, to feel out of the reach of help, in their first year—or even in their first month or their first week together.

What we seriously challenge is a misconception about marriage that, up to now, has been concealed by a haze of rosy idealism. We know well that such a challenge will be highly unpopular, but we are talking about a field in which we have studied and worked for a lifetime, and we don't mind if we are criticized. In our opinion, the time has come to remove the veil and face the truth about the first year—the critical first year—of marriage.

In our years of marriage counseling, we, of course, followed the normal pattern. We took a case history of the couple's shared life. This almost invariably revealed that the present trouble had developed out of mistakes made—in those days almost always as a result of ignorance—in earlier years. Then, when we switched to marriage enrichment, we again found that the troubles the couple had to work through resulted from their failure to develop their relationship as it might have been developed in earlier years. In such cases, the proper thing to do now was to rectify the result of past errors.

Out of this kind of thinking we arrived at the concept of developing the couple's "relational potential." It is common knowledge that we all have capacities to act that are usually never well developed in the course of a lifetime; we don't receive the necessary stimulus to practice them. Our choice of a life career simply means that we plan henceforth to learn a particular set of skills to become expert in that area, and we allow other skills we might have learned to remain undeveloped.

Being a loving and caring marriage partner is made possible by the learning of some relational skills that we now understand and that can be taught, particularly by demonstrating them in action. So, if we choose to marry, we should surely be ready to go through a learning process to develop our inherent potential in that particular direction. The obvious time to begin the learning process, to go through the probationary state, is the first year of marriage.

AFTER THE HONEYMOON, WHAT?

In other words, as soon as the honeymoon is over, the couple should get to work on the task of developing their relational potential. Since skills of this kind are better learned by seeing them in action and practicing them with the cooperation and support of other couples who are in the same learning process, we need to set up programs in which this may be done, under the guidance of leader couples who have themselves mastered these skills and are ready to demonstrate them.

This, then, is what we have tried to plan for newlywed couples. All we have done yet is to make some beginnings. But we are excited about the process, and we are highly gratified about the progress we have made.

In Part IV, we will report to you what has been achieved so far and what we would like to see develop in the future. We dare to hope that this program, if carried out extensively, could lead to a revolutionary change in the quality of marriages.

5

Launching a Program for Newlyweds

Everyone knows that many marriages are getting into serious trouble in today's world. Why is this happening? In an earlier book, we tried to trace the history of the marriage relationship in our Western culture. This meant our reading many big books, but we found it to be an enlightening experience. In our book *The Sacred Fire*, we went back over a period of four thousand years, looking at marriage in the Hebrew culture, in the empires of Greece and Rome, in the Christian era through the Middle Ages to the Renaissance and the Reformation, and up to the present day. The picture this gave us provided a much better understanding of how marriage has developed in our society.

What we saw very clearly was that, for most of our history, the rules about marriage have been firmly set by the Church or the State, and for most of the recent centuries by both together. Why should the State interfere in what we consider to be a private and personal relationship? The reason is very clear: Marriage is the means by which the cultural values are transmitted from one generation to the next. Within the family, the ideals and goals of the culture are passed on—by the parents to the children—and the process continues from generation to generation. We often speak of "human rights" as one of the basic values that democratic governments are pledged to preserve. But we need to remember that the *basic* human right is the right of the child, who will one day become a future citizen, to be guarded, cared for, instructed, and trained in the way of life to which the State is committed. In the past, therefore, both Church and State have combined to control marriage—not for the purpose of interfering in the interpersonal relationship, but to ensure that the couple will faithfully fulfill their duty to care for their children and train them in the principles of effective community living. Failure to do this would endanger the future of the culture, so it has always been regarded as the vital task of the family, and the State has made the necessary laws to see that it is carried out.

Today, however, this ancient system is collapsing because the State has given up its responsibility to hold parents to their duty by allowing easy divorce. We cannot be sure as yet what the final result will be, but at present the divorce rate in the United States threatens too many of the new marriages being contracted. As a result, we are already faced with serious consequences.

Any development that results in better marriages should, therefore, be welcome. The only effective way to make that possible is to enable couples to achieve quality relationships. Sooner or later, Church and State will have to face this fact. If couples can no longer be kept together by external pressure, it will have to be done by making their relationships so meaningful that they will *want* to stay together.

Although the State and the wider public have so far failed to face this fact and to give adequate support to the marriage enrichment movement, this is now one of the most urgent issues concerning the future of every democratic society. At present, this is clearly perceived only by a mere handful of people, but some of us are ready to initiate the beginnings of appropriate action, and are already doing so in the movement for marriage and family enrichment. It is not easy to see any other way in which our values can be preserved in the long-term future.

As we have already explained, we were prompted to launch the marriage enrichment movement because the relationship between husband and wife was changing from a one-vote to a two-vote system, and this was proving much more difficult to manage. We soon discovered, however, that by bringing married couples together in small groups for intensive weekend experiences, we could show them how to develop new ways of interacting that could enable the two-vote system not only to work successfully, but also to produce a much more creative quality of family relationships than we had experienced before on any significant scale. The change was not easy to bring about, and it took time for the relearning process to be carried out. However, the results, in terms of exciting improvements in the quality of family relationships, were rewarding to all concerned.

During the six years after we had started the ACME organization, we were able to train a number of leader couples who, in different parts of the country, led weekend retreats for small groups of four to eight married couples. We found, however, that the retreat experience was not usually enough in itself to bring about a decisive and lasting change in a marriage. When a small group of couples, following the retreat, could be formed into what we have called a "support group," meeting every few weeks in one another's homes, this was usually enough to lead to lasting growth and change for the couples concerned.

Then, in 1979, an opportunity came our way to carry out an experiment in a whole community. In Kansas City, on the invitation of a concerned citizen, Martha Jane Starr, we were appointed consultants in the field of family life. The money was raised for the so-called KC Mace organization to have a small city office with a full-time organizer. Each month, we flew in for about a week and initiated a wide variety of experimental programs for the improvement of family life.

We naturally began with retreats for couple enrichment and in time developed a team of local couples who completed the ACME training for leadership. When this was well established, Mrs. Starr expressed a special interest in reaching newlyweds. This was an opportunity we cordially welcomed, and we saw it as a chance to carry out a daring experiment.

The program was called Growth in Marriage for Newlyweds. It offered the kinds of help which we have already described. The city pastors were given the opportunity to act as recruiting agents, and a number of them responded. The new experimental program began.

Starting with four successive weekly three-hour sessions, the program was so well received that it had to be extended to six sessions, a total of eighteen hours. The couples involved were enthusiastic about it. ACME's proven method of a leader couple sharing with a small group proved to be just right, and in due course a manual was produced to outline the materials included in the program. Mrs. Starr also arranged a series of luncheon meetings to which city pastors were invited and in which the program was explained in detail, so that they might recommend it to couples at whose weddings they were officiating.

Three years after the Kansas City program had been started, a similar program for newlyweds was launched in Winston-Salem by Alice and Hampton Morgan, who had made outstanding contributions to the leadership of the ACME organization. This program followed the general pattern of the one in Kansas City, and it has been equally successful. It was later taken over by another ACME couple, Alvis and Florence Carpenter.

A year later the newlywed program was started in Baltimore by Lyle and Terry Dykstra, a couple who had originally lived in Kansas City and had helped to develop the program there.

Since then, a fourth program has been launched in South Boston, a smaller community in the state of Virginia, where another ACME couple, Bill and Linda McConahey, live. The program is supported by a local fund. A fifth program has been developed in Columbus, Georgia, by ACME members Alice and Richard Robertson.

This account represents the situation at the time of writing, but, of course, we expect various new developments to take place in the future. A more detailed account of the first three of these programs is given later in this book.

Building a Companionship Marriage

6

Why Get Married?
The Critical Question

We see our readers as two people of opposite sexes who are about to embark, or have already recently embarked, on the venture of a shared life. If we ask you why you have planned this, would that be a fair question?

Most people marry, true. But not everyone. The exceptions would be hard to classify—and it doesn't really matter, so we won't try. However, it might be appropriate, as we take up our task, to consider with you briefly just what your particular goals are.

We shall come back to this question in a general way later, when we consider the various aspects of the marriage system. The main purpose, of course, is to continue the culture and its values into the next generation. But that is a *general* purpose. It is, of course, made possible by sexual reproduction, involving a very pleasant experience, and it is normally assured by having a life partner of the other sex to live with.

But is that all? Two parents certainly have a joint task to keep them busy, and the ready availability of a sex partner is very convenient. But is there anything else?

Indeed there is. Two people, living together in the closest intimacy, influence each other in a great many ways. Parenthood makes many demands on them for some years, and sex brings them very close to each other. But neither of these factors now has the importance it once had. In our society, as few as two children should meet the requirement of most couples. Sex is much more widely available in the open society of today, although for the time being AIDS is changing all that.

What, then, is left? The answer is clear: The third need marriage meets is *companionship*. Today, a husband or wife is seen as a life companion. Though this has always been a recognized factor in marriage, today it has become much more important than ever before. This is due to several changes in our modern society.

One of these changes is the new status of women. History may in the future record this as the most significant development of the twentieth century. More and more women are moving out of the limited sphere that they occupied in the past. They are getting education equal to that of men and are sometimes proving to be better scholars. They are entering the world of gainful employment in large numbers and are proving that they have all the ability necessary to succeed in most fields. They are also establishing themselves as men's equals in sports, in entertainment, in exploration, in business, in the professional world, in the arts, and in government. The inevitable result of this vast change is that marriage, for the first time in human history, has become a completely equal relationship— with the one unalterable exception that the wife bears the children, which in these days means little more than a temporary diversion from her other activities.

All these changes involve a profound revolution in the nature of marriage. It has become today, for all practical purposes, a partnership of equals. What this means is that the success or failure of a marriage depends on the achievement of *companionship*. If your marriage doesn't make you good life companions, nothing else can compensate for that failure.

Never before has this been true to the extent that it is true today. A modern marriage that is not an effective working partnership is, by modern standards, not a truly successful marriage.

Does this mean that the modern couple should work, as well as live, together? Certainly this seems to be an advantage, if we judge the question in terms of our own marriage and of a number of other marriages which we know well. Working together for the same goal seems to be a strong uniting process. However, while on the whole a couple's working together seems to be an *advantage*, evidence proves that it is not a *necessity*.

What, then, is the true goal of the companionship marriage? It goes deeper than the world of work or vocation. It has to do primarily, as we see it, with the development of the *personalities* of the two partners involved.

In the early years of life, our parental families play a major role in shaping the kinds of persons we become. Then follows a period when most of us mix freely with a great variety of other people. We are influenced by all kinds of associations, giving us a chance to choose the values that seem most important for us. In due course, out of a variety of alternatives, we settle for the goals that we decide to pursue in the coming years. If all goes well, we choose life partners who either share these goals, or understand and appreciate that they are right for us and are willing to support and help us in our pursuit of them.

Then, in the marriage experience, we agree together

to pursue the goal we have each chosen in a continuing process of growth and change, confident that we will support and help each other as we go through the life span together. Although a common goal for both probably represents the ideal, we cannot expect them always to have a common goal. What really matters is that each life partner is dedicated to encouraging the other to achieve his or her chosen life goal. This, it seems to us, summarizes the meaning and purpose of the companionship marriage of today, which is gradually taking the place of the older forms of marriage that we seem now to be leaving behind.

7

Getting Started—A Challenging Task

Having defined the task of building a companion-ship marriage, we want now to spell out the require-ments you will need as a couple in order to achieve it. Long years of experience in dealing with marriages and in studying what we have learned about close relation-ships, have convinced us that there are essentials that a couple *must* have to succeed. We want to explain these essentials as clearly as we can. Without these basic resources, your chances of achieving a really satisfying relationship are very poor indeed.

Of course, many married couples today continue to live together, after a fashion, and from the outside might give all the appearances of having an acceptable relationship. However, we are writing this book to say that something much better than that is now possible. We are writing for couples who want a deeply satisfying relationship and who are prepared to work hard if necessary to get it. On that basis, therefore, let us proceed.

Please notice that we have started the title of this part of the book with the word *building*. We have done so quite deliberately. We think this provides the best kind of picture to describe the making of a marriage.

We once lived on a street in which, among the houses, there was a vacant lot. After a time, the "For Sale" sign was taken down, and we knew that someone had bought the lot and would presumably be building a house on it. So we began to watch, eager to see what would happen next.

In due course, trucks began to arrive with all kinds of raw materials—bricks, sand, wooden beams and planks, and later windows, doors, and roofing tiles. Workmen then came and, from the untidy piles, began to put the raw materials together to shape them into the kind of home the owners had decided on. As time passed, the finished house gradually took shape, until the family moved in and became our new neighbors.

We want you to keep that picture in your mind and apply it to your present or future task of building a marriage. The similarity between the two operations is a close one.

On your wedding day, photographs will be taken or have already been taken. Imagine a photograph in which you are standing side by side at the altar, facing the pastor, priest, or rabbi. Now add something to the picture that no camera could include. Behind each of you, separately, imagine a pile of boxes and bundles. What *are* these packages? They are all the materials you have gathered together over the years to make each of you the distinct and separate person that you have become, as a result of your earlier experiences of life.

So, what does this mean? It means that once you have become husband and wife and have set off on your new, shared life together, all these piles of packages have to go with you. And now they are no longer two separate piles. Like the materials on the building lot, they have to be skillfully fitted together into one new pile, which will express the shape of your shared life in the future years.

Some of the pieces of baggage you both bring will fit together easily and neatly. Others will have to be juggled around, or trimmed to shape, before they can fit together. Some won't even fit at all, however hard you try, and will simply have to be dumped or replaced by something else.

You can surely see from this practical illustration why we have to talk about "building a marriage." In the light of these practical realities, you can see how Plato's picture of two people who were once joined together and have now found each other and come together again just won't do. Even the highly romantic idea that the state of "being in love" will make the task of joining you together easy and effortless won't work. You just can't avoid the plain fact that, like the workers on the vacant lot, you are confronted, soon after you come down from the altar where you made your vows, with the task of *building* a marriage.

The task, alas, is going to take time and effort. And it is of the greatest importance that you should get started on it soon, in your first year together. It is also important that you understand, as clearly as possible, *how* to go about it.

Unfortunately, in our present culture, you are not likely to be given much training for this task. In fact, so long as the romantic idea that it all happens naturally and effortlessly is allowed to prevail, you may not even understand what you have to do in the first year of marriage.

This is the time when you must get to work on all the complex adjustments and behavior changes you will have to make together if your dreams and hopes are ever going to be fulfilled. As we have already seen, we now know that, if the necessary adjustments are *not* made between you, there is a distinct possibility that you may, as soon as the end of your first year together, find yourselves disillusioned or even alienated.

We must be careful, however, not to represent this task of mutual adjustment as if it were in itself a process of disillusionment, shattering your dreams by bringing you down to a level of hard reality. That isn't the picture at all. On the contrary, as you work on the adjustments you have to make to each other, you should be coming closer together and finding your relationship continually better and more satisfying—just as all the noisy sawing and hammering necessary in the building of a new house are really enabling it to become a pleasant and comfortable home for the family members who are moving in. Every new adjustment you work at together should make you happier and more comfortable—if it doesn't, you haven't done it right!

In this part of the book, then, we want to give you all the information and help we can about the task that lies before you. We have used the idea of building a house, and that is actually a very good way to describe the building of a marriage. Of course, building a house requires a number of people with different kinds of training and much skill. We can't expect the average couple to bring that kind of competence to the building of a marriage. All the same, we take the view that it should be possible in the future to do far more than we are doing now to help couples develop *some* skill in the task of shaping their relationship in ways that will bring them real and lasting happiness together. We will try, in the chapters that follow, to offer you some helpful guidance as you go about this vital task together. We would also urge you, if programs like the ones we shall be describing are offered in your community, to welcome gratefully the opportunity to take part in them.

In the next three chapters, we will try to explain the basic skills you should learn and practice in order to equip yourselves for the marriage building task.

8

Commitment to Mutual Growth and Change

In our traditional culture, when a couple decided to get married, they had to report to a state office or take part in a religious ceremony. The object of this was for them to make a commitment to each other in the presence of witnesses. In the Church ceremony, the words they spoke publicly indicated that the couple would live together "till death do us part." In other words, marriage was being undertaken *for life*.

The reason for this was that, in the eyes of the Church and of the State, the main purpose of marriage was for the couple to have children and that these children would become the future citizens of the nation. Since little was known in those days about birth control, the average marriage produced numbers of children, all of whom had to be cared for and trained for future citizenship. It was, therefore, essential that the married couple should stay together and thus unite in carrying out their joint duty as parents. Divorce was either very hard to get or not available at all.

So marriage was a binding commitment, and for most husbands and wives there was no way out of it. In England until a century ago, the only way to get a divorce was through the passage of a special Act of Parliament in the names of the persons concerned—something available only to a few very influential or wealthy people.

Divorce was easier to get in the United States, but by the standards of the time it was a costly process. Also, public opinion often considered it to be an irresponsible action to take, so it was avoided if at all possible. During this century, however, the requirements for a legally valid divorce have been progressively eased, until we have now reached the point at which the courts have made divorce available almost for the asking. At the same time, public opinion has become much more tolerant, so that today being divorced brings hardly any negative judgment on those concerned. Consequently, it is now estimated that a considerable proportion of all new marriages being contracted today are likely, sooner or later, to end in divorce.

Under these conditions, the commitment to marriage has lost much of its binding power, and increasing numbers of couples see little point in going through a marriage ceremony that has in the past signified a commitment for life. So couples often just plan to live together with no legal or religious ceremony, with the understanding that they can at any time part and go their separate ways. If, however, they make a *private* commitment to each other, that is for them to decide; yet, no commitment is registered in public.

Usually, these couples don't plan at first to have children, which might complicate their situation. Living together is simply a matter of personal convenience to them for as long as they both agree to continue to do so. Either is free at any time to walk out on the other.

In some cases, of course, the couple develop such a mutually satisfying relationship that they decide to stay together permanently. They may at this point agree to become legally married. Their reasoning might be that they now have definite proof that they are well suited to each other and that they are ready to consider having children.

The question raised here is, of course: "When should the couple make *a serious commitment to the relationship?*"

In some cultures, ancient and modern, the commitment has been made by the parents, even before the couple have met each other. As we have seen, in some cases they were married at so early an age that they would have been unable to make a responsible choice. From then on, their marriage was considered as binding for life—unless they failed to produce children, which was generally the test of whether the marriage was valid.

This makes it clear that the question of when a marriage is binding depends on what the culture regards as its primary purpose. As we have seen, the traditional condition was that a marriage was intended, first and foremost, to produce children in order to continue the family line. Today, this is not so important. The modern criterion is that the companionship aspect of the relationship must be well developed, and this may be even more important than all other considerations.

We are now, therefore, in the era of the companionship marriage, because husband and wife today are viewed as equal partners. This may be considered as progress, but it should be clearly recognized that *it makes the task of mutual adaptation to each other much more difficult than it has ever been before.* There can be no doubt that this is the main reason that so many marriages fail today. We have noted that the marriage relationship is now a two-vote system, instead of a one-vote system. The extreme difficulty of settling any issue when the two votes are cast on opposite sides can lead to one deadlock after another. How can any disagreement be settled when the two persons concerned take opposite viewpoints?

It can be done, but it is hard work, and the two partners can soon be arguing against each other. Differences of opinion about how to act in a close relationship can produce crisis after crisis. Either one must give in to the other, and if this happens too often the equality of the relationship is at least temporarily destroyed. They may both insist on having their way, and this produces a deadlock between them. If the issue is one about which both hold strongly different opinions, they may get into a fight. Even that may solve nothing.

These disturbances happen often in the egalitarian modern marriage, and they can easily lead to progressive alienation. This cools the loving spirit that characterizes an affectionate relationship. If it happens too often, the two marriage partners begin to drift apart, because they are either unwilling or unable to work through each crisis until they reach a common mind.

This process of gradual and progressive alienation happens on a considerable scale in modern marriages, and it destroys the possibility of building companionship relationships. The husband may soon feel that his wife is violating his traditional role as the head of the house, and he may begin to assert himself vigorously. The wife will then feel that her rights as a modern woman are being violated. Working this out is inevitably a difficult and time-consuming task. The conditions of many families today, with both husband and wife employed outside the home, leave no time to work through this complex issue. It usually has to be done while both are tired, preoccupied with other matters, and, therefore, unable to examine the situation objectively and arrive at a carefully considered and shared conclusion.

What all this means is that the climate of today's marriages is not very favorable for making the difficult transition from the one-vote (in the appropriately divided areas) to the two-vote (in nearly all areas) system. Yet unless the companionship quality of the relationship is achieved and maintained, progressive alienation can cause the couple gradually to drift apart, to the point at which divorce seems to be the best solution—and it is now so easily available that large numbers of discouraged couples are taking it. What this adds up to is that you need a very serious *commitment* to the difficult task of working together to build a companionship marriage.

What exactly *is* this commitment? We need to be quite specific about it. We call it a *commitment to growth and change*. What exactly does that mean? It means that neither of you is going to continue to be the person you have been. That is true whether you stay married or not. Ten years from now, you will both be different. Your habits will have changed somewhat. Your likes and dislikes will have changed. Some of your values will have changed. Your behavior patterns will have changed.

To sum up, what building a companionship marriage means is that you decide that all your growing and changing will henceforth be done *together*, as a process of getting more and more in tune with each other. Gradually, over time, you will work through your differences in thinking and behaving until many of them are replaced by similarities. Little by little, you will move from isolation to a commonly shared set of standards and values.

Remember, you are going to change anyway. This is an essential element of the process of growing. But because you now live a shared life, you must, if this is to continue and develop, try to do your changing *together*, as much as possible, so that you will be changing *in the same directions*.

This is a complex process, and it won't happen automatically. It has to be agreed on, planned, and worked through by both of you together. It happens slowly and gradually over a period of years. The point is, however, that unless you agree that what you want is a companionship marriage, and unless you get started on it during your first year or soon after, it may never happen at all.

So the question to be settled between you, right now, is: "Have you or have you not agreed that your goal is to develop a companionship marriage? If so, have you made to each other the necessary commitment to shared growth and change?"

9

Building an Effective Communication System

In the year 1967, a counselor called Sherod Miller entered the University of Minnesota, in the Family Study Center, to work on a Ph.D. in family sociology. He had found, in counseling with married couples, that they often had real difficulty in talking to each other about problems that developed in their relationships. Therefore, he wanted to study the field of couple communication. He was joined by another counselor, Elam Nunnally, who wanted to investigate the same subject. Nunnally had found that couples moving into marriage had difficulty in talking freely about subjects like money, sex, and in-laws. Then, in 1969, a third researcher, Dan Wackman, joined the team. Together they worked through all the literature they could find about couple communication and published a 150 page report.

That was the beginning of a movement. The need to help married couples to communicate effectively turned out to be a major challenge. When the three researchers published together a textbook called *Alive and Aware*, over 100,000 copies were sold. The subject of couple communication is still being studied. *Straight Talk*, a popular book written by Carol Saline in cooperation with the three above named researchers, was published in 1981. The subject of couple communication has been written about and taught ever since, and a vast amount of knowledge has now been accumulated and shared. We ourselves, in our marriage, have learned much from these studies. They have brought real improvement to our relationship. We have never ceased to be grateful to the pioneer group who first opened up this field. We got to know them as special friends.

That's all very well, but how much further is this vital new knowledge getting out to married couples? Have you ever heard of the couple communication system, read books or articles about it, taken a course, or heard a lecture? We wouldn't be surprised to learn that you have never heard of it. Somehow we seem to be unable to get most of today's new and exciting information about marriage out to the general public. We've got the answers; yet, marriages go on failing for the lack of the knowledge we have.

It's certainly obvious that you can't build a good companionship marriage unless you can talk about it together. No human relationship can succeed for long unless those concerned can talk freely and naturally about their thoughts and feelings, their hopes and fears, their plans and goals. Two people who live together have to be in communication with each other about their experiences. If their feelings and thoughts can't be communicated on a day to day basis, though the couple continue to live together, they will drift apart in terms of their interpersonal relationship.

So, when we developed marriage enrichment, we saw clearly that one of the basic needs of the couples we worked with was improvement in their communication systems. In fact, we couldn't help them much in other areas *until* we had enabled them to talk to each other.

61

What we found was that married couples communicate with each other at three levels.

The first level is without words, but it is quite important. Most animals of the same species get along together, and that means they have to be able to communicate. They have no words to speak, but they can make noises to indicate that they are happy, in pain, anxious, or frightened. We do the same. Also, both we and the animals can communicate with each other by the way we look and the way we act. All married couples develop a system of signs—facial expressions, waving of the hands, finger pointing, and other body movements.

The second level is the use of spoken words. You can explain something or describe an experience you have had or tell your partner what you plan to do. You can respond to a suggestion positively or negatively. You can discuss a subject in which you are both interested or work out the details of something you plan to do later. You can ask or answer questions.

These forms of communication are freely used by married couples. But there is a third level that may or may not be used. It involves sharing with your partner inner thoughts and feelings that reveal more about you than you generally want other people to know. These are feelings that you consider private or thoughts that you prefer not to reveal or intentions you prefer to keep secret because you feel they would lead to your being judged or threatened or rejected. They concern areas of your inner self that you feel should not be known to other people.

Many married couples confine their communication to the first two levels. That enables them to get along tolerably well. However, the companionship marriage goes also to the deeper levels. This is, of course, a risk, and you may feel unable or unwilling to take it. But opening up the communication system at the deeper level is a vital act of trust that brings great rewards if you are prepared to take the risk.

In marriage enrichment retreats, one of the most common exercises is the leader couple turning to each other and sharing openly some of their personal thoughts about their relationship in a dialogue that the other couples can hear. Then the other couples are invited to turn to each other and, privately, do the same. This often shows couples how important it is for them to feel free to talk to each other about the state of their relationship. You could try this at home together.

Once we as a couple had learned the value of the couple dialogue, we decided that it was something we might do together every day. It enabled us to keep up with each other's inner thoughts and feelings, which we found very helpful.

We have called this our "daily sharing time," and we have kept it up ever since. The time and the place can be decided to suit the couple's convenience. In our case, the early morning, before we start the day, has turned out to be the best time. We are not likely then to be interrupted, and we make it a pleasant occasion by drinking cups of tea, a habit carried over from our British background.

We start each day, each knowing what the other is feeling, thinking, and planning. We share any hopes or fears we may be experiencing as we go out into the new day and give each other encouragement and support. If some major issue or concern comes up in our daily sharing time, we don't try to deal with it then and there.

We schedule a convenient time later when we can be free to explore it fully.

We know many other couples who plan regular sharing times when they can catch up on their communication with each other. They tell us they find this time very valuable. In some cases, they first write down separately what they need to share with each other, and then they share it.

The particular way you plan your time for open and honest communication doesn't matter, *as long as you do it.* What is important is that you share, regularly and honestly, the thoughts, feelings, and wishes you have about yourself and your relationship. A marriage without a regularly functioning communication system just can't develop into a companionship relationship. This is the essential starting point.

10

The Creative Use of Anger and Conflict

The title of this chapter may startle you; it has startled a good many people. Some years ago David wrote a book entitled *Love and Anger in Marriage*, published by Zondervan. Before they read it, people assumed that the book was intended to help couples cope with two opposite emotions—love, which is good and creative, and anger, which is bad and destructive.

But that wasn't what the book was about. It was intended to help couples use love and anger as *both* healthy and creative emotions, which, when rightly used, could cooperate in the building of good marriages.

Does this sound impossible? Well, let us try to explain it, and let us share with you that our discovery of how we could use our anger positively brought about some real growth in our own relationship.

Anger is a strong, positive emotion. It is an immediate, spontaneous emotion that leaps into your awareness when you are threatened by something someone says or does to you that seems like an attack. Swift changes take place in your body chemistry. The process is complicated and happens quickly. You are on the defensive, and your very life may be in danger.

It is fascinating to trace, as we did, all the physical factors that go to work when you are angry. Anger is our basic survival kit. Some people think we are responsible for getting angry, but that isn't true. Anger is an emotion we share with most other living creatures, and it develops below the level of the conscious mind. Therefore, we are not responsible for it.

However, once anger is there, we are responsible for what we do with it. It braces us for action, but we have to choose the best way to act according to the circumstances. The alternatives we have are three: fight, flight, or freeze.

Apply this to a married couple: One gets angry with the other because he or she has done something that seems damaging or threatening. The response may be to fight—a physical blow or a verbal attack. It may be to walk away and refuse to take any action. It may be to feel paralyzed and incapable of any response. Whatever reaction you are likely to make will depend on your natural temperament.

However, this is a crisis, and something must be done about it. As married couples get to know each other, they tend to develop a standard pattern of interaction. Some fight vigorously until the emotional tension dies down. Then for a time there is a period of coolness between them, after which they may talk about the issue and try to clear it up. Alternatively, the couple may lapse into silence or get away from each other until, after a time, they try to behave as if nothing had happened. All kinds of behavior patterns are used in the attempt to get back to the normal relationship.

What seldom happens is that the couple sit down together, analyze what has been going on between them, and finally clear it up. This is more difficult for some people than for others—especially for those who, as we describe it, "lose their tempers."

We are now convinced that we all have the power to decide how we deal with anger when it stirs within us. This decision is made by the conscious mind, and we can learn to change our ways of acting over time.

In marriage, your anger against your partner usually means that you have been hurt. Something he or she says or does is making you feel demeaned or put down, and your angry reaction is a spontaneous act of self-defense. If this can be understood and accepted by both of you, and if you can then both go behind the anger to the hurt feeling, examine it, and clear it up, you have made some real progress.

This isn't easy to do, but it can be learned. Once this has been done, it opens the way for real growth in the relationship. As long as you react to anger either by attacking your partner or by suppressing your hurt feelings, no progress can be made. But once you can share your hurt feelings and ask for understanding and support, it becomes possible to plan together and clear up the situation that triggered the anger in the first place. Then it is not likely to happen again with that particular situation.

Dealing with anger is one of the best ways of coming closer to each other. To fight is to alienate each other. To suppress anger and pretend it isn't there is to evade clearing up the situation and also risks an explosion of accumulated resentment later. To get behind the anger to the hurt that caused it and to clear that up is to remove a barrier to closeness and love.

When we first came to realize this, we found we had a lot of clearing up to do in our own relationship. But once we had discovered how to share a feeling of anger, take time to dig down to the basic hurt that had caused it, and clear that up, we found that the threat of anger no longer troubled us. Indeed, clearing up anger situations turned out to be an exciting opportunity to expand the love and trust in our relationship.

We would go so far as to say that sharing and working through anger situations is a vitally important way of enabling a close relationship to grow. When there is danger that one of the partners might be dominated by the other, anger protects the individuality of both partners. Love can then draw the married couple closer together; of course, the talk about the two becoming one is in the field of poetry, not prose!

A good marriage is a healthy balance between unity and separateness. Love pulls us toward unity, but when this begins to threaten our separateness, anger develops to halt the process and to restore the balance. This avoids the danger of what we call an "enmeshed" relationship, in which one of the partners becomes so closely involved in the other as to lose his or her separateness and independence. This is avoided when anger in the relationship is recognized as healthy and is properly used to maintain the balance.

11

Sex, Money, and In-laws

If this book had been written half a century ago, these three aspects of marriage would have had a central place among the subjects dealt with. The fact that we are dealing with all three in one short chapter illustrates some changes in the modern viewpoint. Let us look at each of them in turn.

Sex

There has never been any doubt about the importance of the sexual relationship in marriage. Marriage as we understand it hardly exists among animals and lesser creatures, although in herds the strongest male may dominate all the females, and birds' pairing off to raise a family is widely practiced.

In most settled human communities, however, the man has the exclusive sexual possession of one or more women, and he fights off all who challenge his right. The reason for this is that he needs to be sure that the children his wife produces, and whom he protects and supports, are really his own.

Over time, the sexual experience, always pleasant for the husband, has come to be seen as also pleasant for the wife. The result is that we have come to see the importance of making it, if possible, equally pleasant for both.

WHEN THE HONEYMOON'S OVER

This led at first to an intensive study, earlier in this century, of what we call "sexual technique." Books were written, giving detailed instructions for the achievement of "mutual and simultaneous orgasm." Couples who couldn't manage to achieve this were made to feel inadequate. It almost seemed that the harder they tried, the more often they failed.

Today, we are coming to see that we may have overemphasized the physiology of sex. We have even called it "making love," with the disturbing implication that if you couldn't do it "by the book," you couldn't really love each other.

We are now developing a broader perspective. The way in which the married couple achieve their sexual relationship is their own exclusive concern. Just how they manage intercourse and how often they have it are purely personal matters between them. Rather than "making love" by coming together sexually, they make their sex life, and its technique and frequency, the expression of the love they have developed in their interpersonal relationship. In a real companionship marriage, therefore, sexual intercourse—the way it is carried out, and how often—is something the couple should be free to decide between themselves, with the same openness and honesty with which they decide all the other aspects of their relationship. It is not so much that in having sex together they "make love" as that developing a real love relationship enables each couple to use their sexuality in whatever way it can best contribute to their mutual happiness.

In other words, they alone must be free to decide just how they can best meet each other's sexual needs. No standard procedure requires them to "measure up" to the general average. If you want to study how others behave together sexually, by all means do so; there is plenty of literature on the subject. But when you have read all you want to read, the two of you must together find whatever pattern of sexual behavior best meets your own personal needs.

Because "being in love" is our accepted condition for getting married, and because "making love" is the term we use to describe sexual intercourse, we might conclude that a good sexual relationship will inevitably guarantee a good marriage. Unfortunately, it is not so simple as that. As a speaker at a medical conference once pointed out, the average frequency of sexual intercourse in marriage is twice a week. If we allow half an hour for each act of intercourse, that equals an hour a week, which adds up to about fifty hours in a year. So the total time devoted to sex is less than the equivalent of one weekend a year! The speaker was not trying to say that the sex life of the married couple is unimportant, but that its value will be greatly diminished if the rest of the year is not spent in building and maintaining an effectively functioning companionship marriage.

Money

In this area, too, many changes have occurred. In earlier times, money was an important factor in the planning of a marriage. Making money on any scale was the prerogative of *the man* in our society. He owned money either because he had inherited it or had earned it by his labor.

Either way, marriage just wasn't available to him until he had enough in the form of savings to buy and furnish a home and an assured income for the future. Very few women, unless they had inherited it, had money enough to live on, let alone to maintain a husband and children. So, in order to marry at all, the man had to convince the woman of his choice and her family members that he could provide adequately for her and any children who might result from their union.

When the couple *did* marry, the custom was for him to manage all the financial arrangements. He paid all expenses connected with the home, and he gave his wife a "housekeeping allowance" out of which to provide the food and other necessities. It was not unusual in those days for the wife to be unaware not only of how much her husband had in his bank account, but also of how much he earned in his occupation!

Contrast this with today's very different situation. Unless the wife marries quite young, she will probably have a job or some other source of personal funds. When the couple marry, they will each be earning separate incomes, and this may continue even while they have children. No longer does the husband have exclusive control of the money to be spent. Both partners must share this responsibility. Since they may differ on such major questions as what furniture to buy, whether to have a new car or an additional car, and how much to spend on a vacation, the whole question of money management can easily become a very controversial issue.

Here, again, the married couple must find a way to resolve many questions—not only how much to spend on what, but also how much to put into savings for future needs. As in the area of sex, books are available to help couples settle the issue of money management. But unless the couple have developed a flexible way of resolving differences of opinion and establishing agreed standards, each financial discussion can become an emotional tug-of-war.

Again, however, this issue can be settled only by agreeing on a pattern of money management that must be worked out by both parties *together*. Doing this will have to be based on how well they have reached agreement on the principles and standards they will honor in their shared life. There is no universally accepted plan for all married couples to use in managing their money. Each couple must work out what seems best in their particular personal circumstances.

In-laws

The coming together of a man and woman in marriage may seem, on the surface, a relatively simple matter. However, it also involves many other people who would otherwise never have "come together." At the wedding, they all attend in high spirits and on their best behavior. They are dressed in their best clothes, and they greet each other cordially.

However, as time passes, tensions may develop. The marriage of a close relative of yours requires you to develop a new relationship not only to someone you have probably never met before, but also to many other people who are members of that person's family.

In the old days, of course, the situation was not so difficult. The marrying couple then were very likely to have lived and met in the same community, and it was probably a small community where everybody knew everybody else and all shared the same ideas about life and the same ideals.

We have no specific statistics on this, but we would guess that today, at most weddings, a high proportion of the attending relatives were total strangers to one another before the couple met, and they would by no means have shared the same philosophy of life.

Today, American society is open, in the sense that people of very different standards and values have learned to live together and to tolerate one another's differences in the same country. However, when a couple marry, they often bring into their union a variety of standards and values from their respective family backgrounds. The couple not only have to adjust to each other as persons, but also to come to terms with some very different ways of thinking and acting. We will deal further with this issue in the chapter on families of origin.

Your First Year Together

12

Off to a Good Start!

In this section of the book, we shall be very practical. We want you to have the best possible chance of achieving a really happy companionship marriage, because we ourselves have had this experience for a lifetime, and we know there is nothing better.

What, then, are your chances of success? They depend, much more than on anything else, on two factors: what you bring to each other in the way of resources and how effectively you use those resources in the process of adjusting to each other.

You may be inclined to think that the first of these will count for more than the second, but we're not so sure. Yes, there are couples who just don't have what it takes and who have very limited chances of succeeding in marriage. But it is definitely our impression that the number of such couples is quite limited.

What is much more true is that *most marriages that fail do so not because the couple don't have what it takes, but because they are unable to make effective use of the adequate resources they possess.* We think this is a great misfortune. You have only one life to live in this world, and it seems a great tragedy to mismanage your closest relationship so that you fall far short of your possibilities. Let us, therefore, look seriously at those possibilities and really work to develop them.

Look at it in this way: *The interactions that take place between two people who have chosen to be close companions are very many, and most of them are quite complex.* If those interactions are wisely developed in your first year together, the chances are good that you will achieve a happy and healthy relationship from the very start. If this happens, it will likely go on like that for a lifetime. If, on the other hand, you mismanage your interactions in your first year together, your relationship could develop problems that will continue with you. These problems could become so habitual that they will be more and more difficult to correct later.

Marriage counseling services have been developed in our culture in recent years, primarily for the purpose of helping couples whose relationships are in danger of falling apart. The reason those couples are in trouble, again and again, is that their earlier years together were not well managed, with the result that stresses and strains have built up over time. Consequently, the task of the counselor is to try to clear up the results of mismanaged relationships. In some cases at least, counseling skills can do this, but only when the couple really work at it long and hard. Wouldn't it have been much better if those couples had done it right from the very start?

That is what we are trying to persuade you to do. In your first year together, you need to start building that house we have been talking about on really firm foundations. Each time you do something wrong and fail to correct it, you are adding to the possibility that the house will rest on shaky foundations, as a result of which it could finally collapse.

All right, you say, what you are telling us makes sense, and we are ready to do what you recommend. Where do we go from here? If it is your sincere decision to go on, let us go right ahead and consider what can be done in your first year of marriage to make sure that the later years will lead to the development of a really sound and lasting companionship relationship.

What, then, are the basic requirements you will have to meet? They can be summarized under four headings. They are:

1. A sincere commitment by each to the other that it is your intention to work together for the growth of a lasting companionship relationship as we outlined in chapter 8.
2. Getting to know each other really well, by going over carefully and thoroughly together your personal histories and deciding on the major adjustments you need to make to adapt to the differences in your ways of thinking and acting.
3. Examining closely your different families of origin to discover what standards and values both of you have, often without realizing it, taken for granted and where you need to readjust your attitudes and share a common purpose.
4. Reaching agreement on your future goals and objectives so that you are of one mind about what you are striving together to achieve during a shared lifetime.

A final note. If as a couple you are already past your first year together, but you want to follow this program, by all means go ahead and do so. It may be a little more difficult, because you may have already formed habits that you will now need to change. But, as the old saying goes, "Where there's a will, there's a way!"

13

Getting to Know Each Other Better

Let us now look at what you are bringing, as separate individuals, to the shared life you are now starting together. This will require your setting aside enough time to talk together in leisurely fashion, if possible in a place where you are not likely to be interrupted. Decide whether it would be best for each of you to take a turn to answer all the questions below, while the other listens, or for you both to answer each question together. Try both ways if you like. Plan enough time for each of you to answer all the questions, which will probably mean getting together for a number of sessions. When you have finished, you should each know the other better than you did before, which will really help in developing your relationship on a secure and lasting basis.

Of course, you already know a good deal about each other, but what we are now doing is filling in some of the details. If there are areas you would prefer not to explore at this time, they can be postponed until later. Obviously, if you are really embarking on a shared life, you will need to know all the significant facts sooner or later.

One of our interesting discoveries in working personally with large numbers of couples is that many of them have never really told each other much about their earlier life and childhood. This information has not been withheld for any particular reason. Yet it should be of real interest to both of you, and it often helps to explain attitudes that could otherwise be puzzling.

Surely it is your intention as a couple to keep up with the events and experiences of each other in the future. Won't this be made easier if you begin by really knowing about each other's basic experiences in the past?

If you agree, then here is a list of twenty questions about past experiences that you might consider sharing with each other. No doubt, you will think of other questions; by all means include them. You might have discussed some of these issues before your wedding. Feel free to elaborate, if you need to, on your earlier comments.

1. How much do you know about the circumstances in which you were born and how you began life *in your very early years?*

2. What do you remember about *your parents* in your early childhood years—how they treated you, how you treated them?

3. What was your feeling about the setting in which you lived in *your first five years*, before you went to school—the house in which you lived; brothers and sisters; other family members; neighbors and childhood friends; other places you visited; significant experiences, both positive and negative?

4. How did you get along in *your younger years in school*—your special friends; your teachers; how well you learned; your special interests and hobbies; any outstanding experiences, positive or negative?

5. How did you get along in *your later school years* as you entered your teens—your special friends of both sexes; how you perceived yourself as an adolescent, compared with the others with whom you shared experiences?

6. What do you remember of *your becoming aware of your sexual nature*—sex as you understood it in your childhood years; early sexual experiences, positive and negative; how you adjusted to your sexuality during the adolescent years; feelings of guilt and feelings of pride? Do you have any concerns about early sex that might affect your sex life in marriage?

7. What do you remember of *yourself as a student?* How well did you do in school? What were your areas of special interest? What did you enjoy reading, and what did you like to read most?

8. What were *your hobbies and spare-time interests?* What did you really enjoy doing? Did you participate in sports, in collecting things, in developing new skills? What are the five things you enjoyed doing most of all?

9. What about *your social relationships* with other people outside your family? What organizations did you join or would like to have joined? Did you enjoy being part of a crowd or with just a few friends? Did you talk a lot or just listen when with other people? Did you have a few special friends? What was your relationship to them?

10. *What chances did you have to travel?* What interested you most? How often did you get away from home? Were they all good experiences?

11. *How did you feel about being all alone?* Did you enjoy

it, or did you feel unhappy and insecure? What are the things, if any, you like to do all by yourself?

12. *Has religion been important to you?* If so, what experiences have been most meaningful? Do you now belong to a church of some kind? If so, is involvement in its activities important to you?

13. *Are you by nature a competitive person?* If so, just what does it mean to you? How important is it for you to *win?* Is it very hurtful to lose?

14. *What do you want to accomplish during your lifetime?* Do you have plans for a special career? Do you want to travel and see the world? What three places would you especially like to visit, and why?

15. *What kinds of books do you most like to read?* Can you explain why they are so attractive to you?

16. *What forms of entertainment are most meaningful to you?* Are there other forms that you just don't enjoy?

17. *What interests and attracts you most in the world of nature?* Do you especially enjoy taking walks; sailing on rivers, lakes, or the sea; studying the habits of birds or animals? What else?

18. *What about your health record?* Have you had any serious illnesses? Are you handicapped in any way? Is there a history of illness in your family?

19. *If you each had the chance to make one change in your physical make-up or in your personality, what would that change be?*

20. *How do you feel about each other's personal vocations—* the work you may do outside the home; careers you may have chosen; your future plans and how they might affect your shared life; your possible future as parents?

A good way to deal with what you discover in this

exercise is to use "the four A's." As you each learn where the other is coming from in one area of living after another, try to decide which of the following represent your major reactions.

1. *Approval.* I'm entirely happy about where you are in that area, so no change needs to be made.
2. *Acceptance.* I can see why you think and act in that way, and I'm willing to support you in what you do.
3. *Adaptation.* Your behavior in that area isn't really what I would prefer, but I understand where you are, and I hope you are willing to make a few small changes.
4. *Adjustment.* Here I can see possible trouble, so we had better plan to work on it together and find a mutually acceptable solution.

If you adopt this policy, you should end up with some areas where, if your relationship is to work smoothly, you will both have to explore together some new patterns of behavior. Arriving at effective solutions in some areas will inevitably take time, but if you both clearly understand what you are seeking together and keep on working at it, the best possible adjustment should finally be worked out between you.

The best plan is to get working on these adjustment tasks early in your marriage. It is necessary to realize that working on them is going to take time. If you are each willing to adjust *some* of your attitudes to the way the other behaves, you should finally be able to make changes that you both can accept. This is the way to lasting happiness.

14

Understanding Your Families
of Origin

As individuals, you both bring to the task of living a collection of qualities, attitudes, and gifts you received from your parents, and in the family from your brothers, sisters, uncles, aunts, grandparents, and cousins. We have discovered, in working with newlyweds, that they often find themselves getting into disagreement and conflict about differences that, although they had not realized it, go back to their "families of origin." For example, the way you eat your meals probably represents the pattern you grew accustomed to during all your years at home. After all, if you ate at home until you reached the age of fifteen, and you had three meals a day, that adds up to a total of over fifteen thousand meals! You each obviously developed some habits and choices that influenced what you like to eat and how you like to eat it! Since you now plan to eat your meals together, some adjustments may need to be made.

You each need to look at the habit patterns you took over from your families of origin to see how far you need to make adjustments in shaping your joint policy for your future years together. Here's another list of twenty questions.

1. What were your eating habits? How were meals prepared and eaten in your families of origin? When

were those meals served, and how did you sit at the table? Did you wait until all were assembled to begin? Did you begin by saying grace? Who set the table, and who did the preparing? Were there definite mealtimes, or were they flexibly arranged? What if you didn't like what was being served? Who talked most during meals, and about what? Did everyone wait until all had finished? Who cleared up after the meal?

2. What were your sleeping habits? Was a regular bedtime enforced for the children? Did you have a bedroom of your own, or was it shared with others? Were you allowed to read before the light was turned out? Had you any special habits about the way you slept? Did you sometimes have bad dreams or nightmares? How were you awakened the next morning? Were there strict rules about keeping your bedroom clean and tidy?

3. Could you bring home guests? What notice was necessary? Could a guest stay overnight? Were guests welcomed by your family? Were you free to go as a guest to another family?

4. Did you have to share in house cleaning? Were there other special jobs you had to do in the home? Did you get paid for helping with the housework?

5. Were there firm rules about when you had to be home in the evening? What happened if you broke the rule? Did your parents make other rules that had to be kept?

6. When you misbehaved, how were you punished? Did you accept this or rebel against it? Did you feel that the rules were fair or unjust? Did you get fair treatment compared with others in the family?

7. How would you rate the marriage of your parents? Were they loving and affectionate? Did they argue with each other or get into fights? Would you consider them good models for your own marriage?

8. Can you think of some situation when your parents were especially kind to you? Were there other situations when you felt they treated you unfairly?

9. What qualities in your father do you feel were especialy good? Were some not so good?

10. What qualities in your mother do you feel were especially good? Were some not so good?

11. How did your parents teach you to manage money? Did they give you a regular allowance? Did they give you a chance to earn what you needed? Did you save up for special things you wanted? Did you have a bank account of your own?

12. Can you remember your parents going through a crisis of any kind in their marriage? What happened, and how did you feel about it?

13. How did you relate to any brothers or sisters in your home? Who were your favorites and why?

14. How did your parents react to your having friends of the opposite sex? Did they make firm rules for you about your dating experiences?

15. Did your parents give you any teaching about sex? Did they make any rules for you about sexual behavior?

16. Did your parents seem to approve of your choice of a marriage partner? Does your partner get along well with them now?

17. What was your attitude to your grandparents? Did you know them well, and did they treat you kindly?
18. What about uncles and aunts and other relatives? Did you have close relationships with any of them, and how did they treat you?
19. Overall, how would you rate your family of origin? Positively or negatively or somewhere in between?
20. How would you rate the family of origin of your marriage partner? Would your partner's rating and your rating be in agreement?

After answering these twenty questions and discussing them, consider together how far your families of origin have shaped your judgment of how to behave in close relationships. Can you see areas where your habitual living patterns, as a result of your earlier training, would be in agreement? Can you see some other areas where the living patterns to which you have been accustomed might clash so that you will need to work out together what you will want as the pattern for your shared life in the future? This has often been a source of problems for married couples, especially when they came from very different backgrounds.

There is one golden rule that all married couples should try earnestly to follow in their relationship to their families of origin. It is: *Try never to allow your family members, or any one of them, to make critical judgments of your marriage, or of your marriage partner, when your partner is not present to hear what is said.*

When this happens, it nearly always causes trouble. Make it clear that you are open to receive helpful suggestions about how to improve your marriage relationship, because that will always be welcome. But you and your partner want to hear such suggestions *together*, so that you can, if necessary, act on them together.

If suggestions about your behavior are, in fact, made by family members on either side to both of you together, always try to treat them seriously. If they seem not to be relevant, nevertheless take the trouble to explain carefully, and positively, why they are not acceptable.

It is worth going to a great deal of trouble for *both* of you to develop good relationships with *both* of your families of origin. They must not be allowed to control your behavior, however, and you should make every effort to have them understand it. A marriage can gain a great deal of support from the families of origin when the couple really try to establish good relationships all around.

15

The Future of Marriage

We want in this chapter to take a look at the prospects for the marriage relationship in our culture in the coming years. Some people are saying today that we are witnessing the end of marriage and family life. They even suggest that the State will have to take over the task of rearing children and preparing them for adulthood. This would be a formidable task. But quite apart from that grim possibility, we personally see some hopeful signs for the future of families.

We all know that marriages are failing today on a scale seldom seen before. That is obvious to everyone, but what few people realize is that, on a much smaller scale at present, and never recognized or reported, some marriages are *succeeding* as marriages have never succeeded before. We would venture to guess that these might be about 10 percent of the total and that the number is slowly increasing.

We must remember that our modern concept of the companionship marriage was probably almost unknown in the past. As we have noted, until quite recently, marriage was strictly controlled by both the churches and the legal system. A basic part of that control was that divorce was either not allowed at all or was allowed only for extreme reasons. So married couples were literally locked together for life. Whether they were happy or not was no one's concern. Their job was to rear their children and thus to continue the culture into the next generation. Once married, they had no real alternative.

In the course of a century, nearly everything has changed. We now have the sexual revolution, birth control, the emancipation of women, fathers deserting their children, and unconditional divorce. All these dramatic events, with other social changes, have combined to shatter the locked-in marriage pattern of the past and have created great confusion.

Along with these changes, however, has come something else quite new: the concept of marriage as a *lifelong companionship of equals*. This new relationship, uniting two people of differing sexes in a profound sharing of mutual support throughout the life cycle, is raising interpersonal growth and deep and lasting relational fulfillment to levels of quality rarely experienced in earlier times.

So today's couple are being presented with a choice—to stay with the old system and hope to make something of it or to choose the new system and work hard to achieve it. That is the choice we offer you, as a couple entering marriage in today's world. If you choose the old system, it may turn out all right for you—or it may not. If you choose the new system, you'll have to take it seriously and work hard to achieve it. It would be wise for you to get in touch with other couples who are making the same choice and who will give one another the help and support they and you may need. The numbers of those committed to the companionship marriage are small so far, but all the evidence suggests that the "marriage enrichment movement," as we call it, is steadily increasing as it becomes better known.

As we write this, we are now at the point of being ready to move ahead. The programs for newlyweds, which we will describe in the following pages, have given us encouragement, and we now feel that we know what to do.

We still believe that both marriage education and marriage counseling are vitally important services, and they have our full support. But we now want to see something new added. What we want to see is *a national movement to provide programs for newlyweds in as many local communities as possible.* We now know how to run these programs successfully, and we want to see more and more communities begin to offer them.

Just how these programs should be developed will become clear as we gain further experience. However, in about ten years of experimentation, we have already learned a great deal. We believe that leadership of the program should always be by a married couple who can demonstrate a working model of a companionship marriage and who have been through the program of training and certification that ACME has developed over a period of now about fifteen years in a number of different countries.

We have come to the conclusion that this program will work best when the qualified leader couple spend an extended period of time with a group of not less than four and not more than eight newlywed couples in their first two years of marriage. While some teaching is appropriate, we have found that the best learning comes when the leader couple dialogue openly in the group. The newlywed couple are encouraged to talk with each other, privately at first, with the possibility of voluntary open discussion later if they are willing.

The basis of the learning process is thus *experiential*. In other words, the couples may "learn by doing," either in the group or privately at home between meetings. However, nothing is required of the participating newlyweds at the first stage other than their hearing the message and watching the leaders as they demonstrate what they teach.

How can this be organized? Already in the communities where ACME has offered programs we have found effective ways to do it, and further experimentation will no doubt open up other possibilities. The principles we have applied so far have been based on findings of the behavioral sciences, which in recent years have done considerable research on couple interaction. As we learn more, in theory and in practice, we shall no doubt be able to make our programs even more effective.

However, we have already done enough testing to know that our present programs are effective. It should now be possible to extend them to more and more communities. The ACME organization, which we hope our reader couples will join, is now ready to develop further programs in communities that are prepared to offer what we consider to be the necessary conditions. We strongly favor the development of an ACME chapter in the community, and the selection, training, and certification of suitable leader couples, before a local program is launched.

While ACME favors beginning with newlywed couples, we have also developed considerable experience in working with groups of couples in other stages of the marital life cycle. All our programs are led by certified leader couples who have been through our selection and training process. All our programs are for married couples who want to develop their relationship by developing what we call their "marital potential."

In the next part of this book, we shall tell the story, in detail, of how ACME has been working with newlywed couples over a period of some ten years and just how our programs have been received.

Reports on Three
Programs for
Newlyweds

16

How It All Got Started

While this book seeks to promote a new idea—guiding newlyweds through their critical first year together—we want to make it clear that we have already been testing this out over a period of ten years in five different communities of the United States. The following reports were prepared in 1985, but have not been published until now. We wanted to test the program thoroughly before making it widely known.

We have already explained how, back in 1962, we started leading weekend retreats for small groups of married couples, not couples in trouble, but some who were willing to learn how to make their marriages better. As we worked with these couples in an atmosphere of mutual trust, it soon became clear to us that in many of these marriages a process of deterioration had already started, which we knew could lead later to serious trouble.

However, we found that we could stop this deterioration by training the couples to use new skills in effective communication and in conflict management. In other words, we developed a *preventive* program, which enabled these couples to make their relationships much more satisfying. This was what we called "marriage enrichment." It led us in 1973 to form ACME, the Association for Couples in Marriage Enrichment, now an international organization.

HOW IT ALL GOT STARTED

As we continued to experiment with our marriage enrichment programs, it became more and more clear to us that the earlier we could reach married couples, the more effectively we could train them in the skills needed to achieve the companionship marriages that are more and more favored today, but that are based on a two-vote system, and are, therefore, more difficult to manage.

We decided to try out marriage enrichment programs for newlyweds. An opportunity to do this came our way in Kansas City, where we had been appointed consultants in the field of family life on the initiative of a concerned citizen, Martha Jane Starr.

In 1978, therefore, the Growth in Marriage for Newlyweds Program was launched in Kansas City. ACME-trained leader couples were given special further training to lead these programs, and local pastors joined in and became the recruiting agents. Most important of all, the newlywed couples who went through the program were enthusiastic about it. Starting with four successive three-hour sessions, it was soon extended to six sessions—a total of eighteen hours. ACME's proven method of a leader couple sharing with a small group of participating couples was used.

Three years after the Kansas City program was started, a similar program was launched in Winston-Salem and proved to be equally successful. A year later the program was also launched in Baltimore. Beginnings in other cities have followed.

We have kept in touch with these programs by hearing reports from those who operated them. In 1985, Martha Jane Starr, who had so strongly supported the development of the Kansas City project, invited us to return there and see for ourselves what was happening. This we did in the month of July, and we were so impressed that we decided also to examine the other two programs. We visited Winston-Salem in August and Baltimore in September. What follows is a fairly detailed account of what we found.

17

The Program in
Kansas City, Missouri

We spent one week examining the Kansas City program for newlyweds. We met with some of the city leaders who had encouraged and supported the project; with a number of the ACME certified leader couples who had led the eighteen-hour programs; and with a number of the couples who had participated. We saw these newlywed couples separately for intensive interviews, lasting one and a half hours each. This included an in depth investigation, with their consent, of their present relationships.

Copious notes were taken of all the events during our Kansas City visit. Reports of all meetings with local groups were kindly prepared by Doris Thompson. She, with her husband Jerry, had played a leading role in the development of the program from the very beginning.

Several meetings were held with community leaders, who represented the churches, the social and service organizations, and the Family Study Center at the University of Missouri in Kansas City. The general opinion was that the program had been timely, well operated, and highly successful.

The procedure was that pastors of churches in the city were encouraged, in addition to their customary premarital programs with couples whose weddings they conduct, to try to sign up these couples for the Growth in Newlyweds Program. When it started, the cost of the program was assessed at forty-five dollars per couple. The church in which the couple were married contributed ten dollars and a city fund raised by Martha Jane Starr contributed another fifteen dollars. These figures have varied over time, but the principle involved is that the couple are made aware that both the church and the city have their interests at heart, and this is signified by the contributions they make.

When a couple sign up for the program, a central office is notified. At first this was in the Living Center, which organized preventive programs. It was later incorporated in the Family and Children's Service organization.

ACME member Phyllis Michael, the organizer, made contact with all the registered couples (the total by 1985 was over three hundred) and fitted them into a program in accordance with their wishes. The size of the groups followed the ACME standard—a maximum of eight couples and a minimum of four. When enough couples were ready, a suitable date and location were decided on, a leader couple allocated, and the arrangements completed. The location was often a church; an attempt has been made to plan programs in different areas of the city to suit as far as possible the convenience of the enrolled couples.

The leader couples, all ACME certified with special further training for this particular program, are entitled to their expenses plus a modest honorarium. (ACME takes care not to encourage mercenary motives!)

We met a number of these leader couples—sometimes several together or separately at other times, such as when sharing a meal. All expressed satisfaction and often enthusiasm. They reported on various aspects of the program and shared some of their experiences. Two issues came up several times: the wisdom of disrupting the group interaction policy to show a film (acknowledged to be a very good film) on the sexual aspects of marriage and the increasing awareness of the great importance of the "families of origin" in influencing (often unconsciously) the attitudes and behavior of newlywed couples.

Our most significant experience, however, was the interviews with the couples themselves. The schedule allowed for seven interviews of an hour and a half each, with couples selected to cover each year of the program since its beginning. One interview had to be canceled, but the other six provided significant insights. The plan had been to take full notes of these interviews, with the permission of the couples concerned. This meant one of us conducting the interview while the other took notes. We decided not to make tape recordings in order to free the couples from any uncomfortable awareness that their spoken words were being recorded.

Since we wished to use a standard pattern for all future interviews with couples who had taken part in newlywed programs, we prepared this list carefully in advance. With minor variations, we have followed it closely in every case.

A. Initial Questions

1. Do you feel entirely comfortable about this interview? If not, would you like any change made?
2. Have either or both of you been married before?
3. How long had you been married when you began the program?

4. How long has it been since you completed the program?

5. Did you receive any kind of premarital counseling, or anything similar, *before* your wedding? If so, we would be interested in hearing about it.

B. Reactions to the Newlywed Program

1. When did you first hear about this program?
2. What was your initial reaction to the idea?
3. Why did you decide to get into it together?
4. How did you feel when the time came to start?
5. What was your impression of the first session?
6. What parts of the program helped you most?
7. What parts helped you least?
8. What was your overall impression of the leader couple?
9. What did you learn that was really new?
10. Was anything important not included?
11. Did you feel free to discuss the experience together between sessions or to talk about it to other people?
12. Looking back now, what is your overall impression of the experience?

C. In-depth Examination of the Marriage

The discussion of the first two sets of questions generally took an hour. At that point we asked them whether they would feel comfortable about looking at their marriage in-depth with us. If not, for any reason, they were free to leave.

All the couples agreed to stay for the extra half hour.

We suggested that we might first look at where they stood with regard to what ACME calls the "three essentials" for a good marriage.

1. Commitment to ongoing growth and change.
2. Couple communication—openness to each other.
3. Making creative use of anger and conflict.

They were all comfortable with exploring their relationships at these levels, which they had learned about in the program. What they described were healthy, growing marriages, with none of the usual problem areas. They talked freely about their interaction patterns, and used the couple dialogue spontaneously in the process.

D. Each interview ended with two final questions.
1. If the need should ever arise, would you freely and comfortably seek marital therapy? All replied, without hesitation, that they would.
2. Have you become ACME members, or do you belong to any other support system for couple growth? All replied in the affirmative.

Who *were* these couples? They were selected, at our suggestion, primarily to represent each of the six years covered by the program in order to see whether its effect seemed to be lasting. We were aware, of course, that they were not likely to be a representative sample. They would, however, reflect whether the program had a positive effect on the participants and whether that effect, under favorable circumstances, was likely to continue over time. The answers to these questions were unhesitatingly in the affirmative. The impression all the couples made was entirely positive.

18

The Program in Winston-Salem, North Carolina

In August, 1985, we spent six days in Winston-Salem with a focus on the ACME newlyweds program, which had been in operation there for three years. The program had been developed initially by Alice and Hampton Morgan and then taken over by Alvis and Florence Carpenter. It had been financially supported over the first three years by the Winston-Salem Foundation, and it was given overall supervision by the local ACME chapter. In the three-year period, sixty-five couples had taken part in the program.

On our first evening there, we met with most of the leader couples who had been involved, together with other local people, in supporting the project. We learned that twenty-three churches and fourteen clubs and organizations in the community had participated.

The next two days were spent in interviewing a total of seven couples and taking full notes. Each interview was timed for an hour and a half. From these interviews, we found that, of the fourteen persons involved, five were in second marriages and one in a third marriage. We had found a few such couples in Kansas City, but the proportion here was decidedly greater.

It is clear that the newlywed program has a special significance for people who have failed in an earlier marriage. Such people go into a new relationship with

104

considerable anxiety and are eager to get all the help they can in order to avoid another failure. Several of them talked about the state of abysmal ignorance in which they had been in their first marriage. They spoke with enthusiasm of what it meant to have gone through the newlywed program.

We found that all the Winston-Salem couples had been invited to write, after the event, saying what the experience had meant to them. Of the twenty-four who responded, seventeen used the term "better communication"; eight spoke of how they had learned to manage their conflicts constructively; and seven testified to the help they had gained from being able to share their marital experiences with other couples in the group.

We followed the same procedure with these couples as in Kansas City. All seven of them agreed to take part in an in-depth examination of their relationships. Here are their responses to some of our questions.

1. *Before the wedding, did you receive premarital counseling in any form?* The replies varied from none at all to quite extensive programs. All had been married by ministers of religion, who had been decidedly more concerned with preparation when a second marriage following divorce was concerned.

2. *How do you perceive the task of marriage?* It was very clear that, with a few exceptions, they had gone into the relationship with inadequate concepts of what was involved in adjusting to a shared life with another person. Again and again they referred to the learning that had come to them in the program as bringing them completely new understanding of how to manage a close relationship.

WHEN THE HONEYMOON'S OVER

3. *In marrying each other, did you make a commitment to ongoing growth and change?* Most of them admitted that the idea of marriage as something to be *worked for* and *achieved* had not played a significant part in their thinking until this was made very clear in the newlywed program.

4. *Do you see couple communication as a skill needing to be learned?* A few of them had known about this before the wedding, but most of them had taken it seriously only as a result of what they learned in the newlywed program. All of them were now actively seeking to improve their communication systems.

5. *How well are you dealing with conflict and anger in your relationship?* Again, it was mainly in the newlywed program that they had found out how to avoid either suppressing their anger or getting into fights. Several of them were still having difficulty in this area, though they all now believed they were making progress.

6. *If you ever got into serious trouble in your marriage, would you feel able to seek outside help and to go for marriage counseling if necessary?* They all replied unhesitatingly that they would. The newlywed program had shown them clearly that knowledge is available to couples who can't find the answers for themselves.

7. *Have you been able to talk about your marriage relationships with other couples?* The general opinion was that only through the newlywed program had they been able, for the first time, to discuss their relationship with others. More than half of them, however, had followed up the newlywed program

by joining ACME and getting into support groups with longer-married couples. All who had done this expressed enthusiasm about how helpful the experience had been.

8. *What are the significant areas in which you have gained new knowledge and insight since you enrolled in the newlywed program?* The most frequently mentioned areas were: the significance of behavior patterns learned (often unconsciously) in their families of origin, which led to difficulties and conflicts in their shared life; the great importance of effective communication in avoiding misunderstandings as they interact with each other; the fact that many of the obstacles to a happy marriage represent unwillingness in the partners to make behavior changes in order to adapt to each other; and learning the difficult task of using anger creatively as a means of identifying unmet needs in the relationships.

Our meeting with these couples confirmed strongly our belief that the newlyweds program offers a very important opportunity to share our new knowledge about marital interaction with couples at what Robert Havinghurst called "the teachable moment." The clear implication is that this program should be further developed and extended.

19

The Program in Baltimore, Maryland

This, the most recent of the three programs we investigated, had been in operation for only two years. It was started by Lyle and Terry Dykstra, a couple who had earlier helped to develop the Kansas City program. When they moved to Baltimore, they soon started an ACME chapter and then developed a newlywed program. Lyle, a Presbyterian minister, got the churches involved. Terry, who was then a staff member of the Family and Children Society, organized the project. The local newspaper, the *Baltimore Sun*, joined in and gave wide publicity to the new program.

Our visit to Baltimore was in September and covered six days. This program was very like those we had planned in the other two cities, but it also included a public meeting, which was very well attended. We also had an evening with the leader couples, all ACME certified, who were carrying out this program.

As in the other cities, we scheduled interviews with eight couples who had participated. One interview was canceled. We followed exactly the same process as before. Again we took copious notes and made it clear that nothing reported to us would be identified with the couple concerned. The responses, from fourteen people, were so much like those in the other two cities that we decided to list the exact words they used. By this means we are able to report just what was said, but with no personal identification. Here are their responses to our questions in their actual words.

1. **How did you get into this program?**
   "Reading a newspaper article." (three responses)
   "Our minister suggested it." (two responses)
   "Our church paid part of the cost." (two responses)
2. **How did you respond when you heard about it?**
   "It seemed a good idea; so we decided to try it."
   "We welcomed this kind of help."
   "We were enthusiastic—it was a great idea."
   "We liked the idea of learning new skills."
   "We were very interested."
   "A little apprehensive, but we wanted to gain new insights."
   "We were really excited."
   "It sounded interesting."
   "We wanted to learn more."
   "We decided to go while our marriage was still healthy."
3. **What was your reaction to the first session?**
   "A little uncomfortable—the others were much younger."
   "It was very concrete and down to earth."
   "We felt very warm."
   "We were cordially welcomed by the leaders."
   "A little nervous at first."
   "We settled in quickly."
   "The leader couple spoke from experience."
   "We were afraid we might be asked to speak, but we weren't!"

"It was helpful, but we were struck by the diversity of the group."

"The leaders made us feel very comfortable."

4. **What in the program helped you most?**

"The material about communication." (six responses)

"The part about our families of origin." (four responses)

"Learning about conflict resolution." (four responses)

"The experience of sharing as a couple." (four responses)

"The sex film." (two responses)

"We got some new ideas." (two responses)

"How to negotiate."

"Affirming each other."

"Dialoguing with other couples."

"The modeling of the leader couple."

"Learning how to deal with stress."

"The idea of a daily sharing time."

"The homework between sessions."

5. **Have you any criticisms of the program?**

"The sex film—we knew it all."

"The film should come earlier."

"Even six sessions were not enough."

"Not enough on anger."

"People in the group didn't talk much."

"The illustration of conflict resolution was too minor."

"Nothing was unhelpful." (six responses)

6. **What did you learn that was really new?**

"Couple communication." (three responses)

"Families of origin." (two responses)

"Conflict resolution."

"The daily sharing time."
"The use of exercises."
"The biology of sex."
"The importance of affirmation."
"We learned a lot."

7. Was anything not included?
"Couples having children." (two responses)
"Money management." (two responses)
"A list of places to go for help."
"Children and the wife's career."
"In-law relationships."
"Marriage break-up experiences."
"Marriage in different age brackets."

8. Looking back, what is your evaluation now?
"A very good program."
"Would highly recommend it to others."
"It meant a lot to us."
"It gave us a clear sense of direction."
"The leaders were very warm and genuine."
"It should be made available to many others."
"A very important program."
"We have adopted much of the program material."
"We have made a commitment to have a much better marriage."
"We enjoyed it very much."
"We think it should be offered to all couples early in marriage."
"It brought us reassurance that our experiences were not unusual."

9. What was your opinion of the leaders?
"They were very good."
"Their role playing was enlightening."
"We were impressed by their openness."

"It was breathtaking."

"They weren't didactic at all."

"They were ready to make themselves vulnerable."

"A warm, loving couple."

"They did a good job as facilitators."

"They opened up their own experiences in early marriage."

"During the course the leaders kept rediscovering their marriage."

"They were very good leaders."

"They were very honest and obviously involved in making their own marriage as good as possible."

"They worked together very well."

"We would recommend them to other couples without hesitation."

"The husband was especially good—very easy to talk to and definitely caring. This came through in all he said."

"They obviously cared about each other, listened to each other, and modeled what they were talking about."

"I thought they were excellent—very sincere and modeled and dialogued well."

"They were extremely warm and genuine."

20

Looking Ahead

Including preparation and writing up our reports, this enterprise took about a month of our time. But it was time very profitably spent. It confirms strongly our idea that the first year of marriage is a time when couples need help and when they can use the right kind of help very profitably. In fact, it convinced us that this may prove to be the most important opportunity we have to cut back on our present tragic divorce rate.

We make no claim that the couples we interviewed were necessarily typical of all newlyweds. The fact that they signed up for the program shows that they were open to new ideas. But their enthusiasm about what they learned strongly suggests that many other couples, once they really understood what they were being offered, might have exhibited the same initial interest and the same satisfied enthusiasm.

The negative cultural attitude to the idea of guiding newlyweds through their first year together is dominated by what we call the "intermarital taboo"—a belief that what happens in your marriage relationship is strictly private and must never be talked about with other couples. We think this compulsive defense of privacy probably developed when married couples lived close to each other in small rural communities. In our developing urban culture today, this attitude is preventing couples from learning the complex skills necessary to achieve success in the companionship marriage, and it is depriving them of the opportunity to learn from and support each other.

We feel that the venture into newlywed programs has opened an exciting door of opportunity that, when wisely and extensively used, could cut back on our disturbingly high rate of marriage failure. If the findings of our experiment, reported here, are accurate, the sooner our communities develop this new program the better for their future health and happiness.

Credit must go to the ACME organization for venturing into this new field. It was made possible by the fact that marriage enrichment was willing to break through the taboo in order to focus attention on improving the quality of the marriage relationship.

There are people who are saying today that our whole marriage and family systems are breaking down and will in time have to be replaced by something else. We beg to differ. It is true that marriages are failing today on a scale previously unknown. But as we have said, the evidence being quietly accumulated by the marriage enrichment movement suggests that at the very same time, though as yet only on a small scale, some marriages are *succeeding* today on a scale previously unknown.

Some Conclusions and Recommendations

1. Newlywed programs are warmly welcomed by at least some couples and probably would be by many more if the programs were readily available.
2. There is a special need to focus on training inexperienced couples in effective communication,

in conflict resolution, and in learning to understand how their behavior is influenced by their families of origin.

3. These programs are especially helpful to couples who have failed in previous marriages.

4. We believe the effectiveness of these programs is based on couple leadership and on couple group sharing. We doubt whether a lecture type of program would be nearly as effective.

5. The intermarital taboo, which prevents couples from sharing their experiences of marriage with each other and from giving each other help and support, is a serious barrier to the development of effective marriages in our culture.

6. We look to the time when well-planned newlywed programs can be made available in every community that values good family life.

Some Future Possibilities

We consider that the ACME organization, as it develops local chapters across the country, should try, with the support and help of the communities concerned, to develop not only newlywed programs, but also a number of other new services in the field of marriage and the family. We issue a challenge to such communities to aim at balancing all their family services equally between remediation and prevention—half each of all money and time spent and half each of all personnel employed. We see this as the only way to cut back on the appalling number of families in serious trouble, by offering those families, at earlier stages, skilled training to enable them to keep out of trouble.

We see this as being done at a series of critical points in the marital life span, as follows.

1. Enabling premarital couples to assess in advance the tasks that will confront them, if they do marry. Recent studies make it possible to predict their chances with a high degree of accuracy.
2. Programs for newlyweds as described in this report.
3. Guidance for the couple as they prepare for the arrival of their first child.
4. Helping couples prepare effectively as their children approach the crisis of adolescence, which is also a crisis for many marriages.
5. Enabling couples to manage the transition period from the "empty nest" to retirement.
6. Making marriages creative in the later years.

We see the possibility of organizing community programs in these key areas, on an experimental basis, during the next ten years. Although enrollment in such preventive programs may be slow at first, we see strong support developing as the effectiveness of the programs is demonstrated.

Finally, our ACME experience in the past fifteen years has convinced us that these programs, wherever possible, *should be led by happily married couples* who can demonstrate what they teach. These programs should consist of a minimum of formal teaching and a maximum of practical demonstration based on couple group interaction and support systems.

How could programs of this kind be financed? We think the couples themselves (or their parents, in the case of newlyweds) could be expected to make an appropriate contribution. Also, churches might contribute a part of the cost as an evidence of their ongoing interest in the couples. Further, we feel that Kansas City made a significant gesture by raising a fund to indicate the genuine concern of citizens in the quality of marriages in their community.

The cost of operating these programs need not be heavy. We see no reason why fees should be paid to anyone other than the organizers of the programs. While all couples who lead these programs should go through a process of selection, training, and certification—such as ACME has always required of its leader couples—they should regard their participation in the programs primarily as a form of community service.

When situations develop in which couples in these programs obviously need skilled professional help, the leader couple should be trained to make an appropriate referral to a suitably qualified therapist. ACME has always required this of its leader couples, and it seems to have worked very well.

The address of the national ACME office is:

The Association for Couples in Marriage Enrichment
502 North Broad Street
Winston-Salem, North Carolina 27101

The local telephone number is 919-724-1526. The national number is 1-800-634-8325.

Making a Marriage Assessment

Newlyweds, we want to end this book on a positive and practical note. As we have explained, this book has been put together out of the leadership experiences of seven different married couples. All of us have been involved in "marriage enrichment." And all of us, as a result of what this has meant to us in our own marriages, have reached out to newlywed couples and have tried to help them start right. We wanted them to be able to do what we had done, to appropriate what we called our "relational potential."

So we came together for a long weekend to plan how the book should be written. We wanted to find a way to help you and other newlywed couples build the kind of quality relationships we were enjoying. First, we shared what we had learned in our own experience. Then we tried to put it all together in the form of a book for you to read.

We are now inviting you to join us. Out of our own shared experience, we have tried in this book to tell you how to get started.

Is it worth all that effort? We who have done it are in no doubt whatever about the answer. We would say, with deep conviction, that nothing we have ever worked at has been more rewarding, more worthwhile. Our happy marriages are the most valuable of all our possessions, and working together to find that happiness has been our most satisfying achievement.

It will take effort, and it will take time. But the first important step is to go beyond thinking and hoping and dreaming to *get started*.

Reading about how to be happy in marriage is just not enough. Thinking about it is not enough. Talking about it together is good, but is still not enough. A happy marriage, as we have tried to explain, is something you have to *build*. That means you must agree to get into *action*. Even acting is not enough, unless you *act together*. Even then, it must be the *right kind of action*. Not only must you *start* in action together, but also you must *go on and on together over time*.

By way of doing something really practical, therefore, and making a start, we invite you now to make together what we call a "marriage assessment." How do you go about it? It is done by looking carefully at all the resources you bring to each other and then trying to calculate how you can make the best possible use of them.

Remember, though, that few couples, if any, can expect to have a perfect marriage; we are not even sure that such a thing exists. However, each couple can calculate their "marital potential"—their capacity for achieving the most successful marriage relationship of which they are capable.

Unfortunately in our present culture, very few couples come anywhere near to developing their relational potential to the full. Yet if in any other part of life over which we have equal control we made no more effective use of the potential we have, we might regard this as a major misfortune—even a tragedy.

The reason for this unhappy state of affairs is that,

although the behavioral sciences today are making a great deal of progress, we have not yet developed the necessary skills to apply our new knowledge in detail to real life situations. When we try to do so with married couples, up to now our main approach has been to work only with those who, usually as a result of ignorance, have landed in disastrous situations from which it can be quite hard to rescue them.

This policy is so illogical that it is bound to change over time, so that we can at last sweep away the useless taboos with which we have surrounded the marriage relationship. We hope this will happen early in the next century. But there is no reason for today's young people to wait until then, when we have the necessary knowledge here and now.

So, let us invite you, if you are willing, to take a few steps toward making your "marriage assessment."

This may sound like something technical, but it isn't. You have decided to share your lives together in the closest of all human relationships. Unfortunately, this is a complicated undertaking. It involves a variety of possibilities, both positive and negative. These may, in the future, be measured by undergoing technical tests of your resources. But at the present, most couples can use their best judgment together. That is what we are suggesting to you right now.

A good way to go about this is to write down individual opinions on paper first, doing this separately, and then sharing the opinions together. If you don't want to go to this trouble, just sit down in a place where you are not likely to be interrupted and talk together about your relationship as it has developed up to the present. It might be a good idea for you to agree in advance not to pass judgment on each other's opinions until you have looked at everything together with open minds. Some disagreements will almost certainly arise, but that doesn't really matter. Your purpose will be to look at them closely and work on them until you can reach a conclusion that is acceptable to both of you.

Four areas of your relationship will need to be examined—two positive and two negative.

1. What are the *promising* qualities you both seem to share? Which are contributing positively to the development of a happy companionship relationship *at the present time?* These are the things you both feel good about *right now* and that seem to promise happiness as you look into the future. They are your positive assets. Make a list of them.
2. What other factors in your relationship hold out the promise of good times together *in the coming days*—plans you hope to carry out; circumstances that seem to be favorable; hopes you both share for your future together?

Now be ready to face any negative factors. We all have some!

3. Face any difficulties and disadvantages that seem to stand in the way of your shared happiness—now and in the future—but which you feel reasonably confident you can manage, together, to overcome and to prevent from threatening the quality of your relationship. These may be differences in your temperaments or in your life goals that could make it hard for you, though not impossible, to reach agreement. They are difficulties you could reasonably hope to overcome in time.
4. Finally, you need to face honestly any more serious differences that could take you off in opposite

directions—such as life goals that you don't fully share or opinions that clash and seem unlikely to be reconciled. Disagreements of this kind can be threatening to people who want to live a shared life, and it is often very difficult to accept them. However, they exist in nearly all relationships, and it is much better to face them than to evade them.

We believe that a marriage assessment, which brings these four sets of issues out into the open, is a good step to take as early in the relationship as possible. We consider it wise to be realistic about these issues and to begin working seriously on them during your first year together. Indeed, it would have been wise to examine your relationship in these areas even before marrying at all. When you do marry, to drift through the first year without making any assessment of the factors, positive or negative, that are vital for the future development of your shared life represents very poor planning.

Yet this is precisely what is happening to many couples today, again and again. The persistent overemphasis on romantic love as the basis for a lasting marriage simply doesn't face the facts. In the past, when couples were locked up together for life and the only real test of a marriage was whether or not it produced children, the quality of the relationship could be largely ignored unless it led to extreme results. Today, the quality of the relationship decides, again and again, whether the marriage continues at all. Even more important, it determines whether any children produced are going to have a fair chance of developing into mature and responsible future citizens.

We hope that we shall soon be able, in the services we provide, to shift our focus from the heavy present emphasis on the rehabilitation of families who, largely as a result of ignorance, have developed all kinds of relational problems with disturbing social consequences. We need to focus our attention on the couples *now moving into marriage,* providing them with all the guidance, support, and help they need as they embark on a relationship that has such vast implications for their personal happiness, for the health of our social system, and above all for the future of our culture.

So, please, for your own sakes and for the sakes of all others concerned, before you lay this book aside, consider seriously making together a marriage assessment.

Now we must bid you farewell. Our wish for you is that, as the years pass and as you continue to work on the exciting and rewarding task of building the deeply satisfying relationship you both want and need, you will experience the same mutual fulfillment that we, your authors and friends (fourteen of us!), are now enjoying.

APPENDIX 1

Authors and Contributors to This Book

The authors, David and Vera Mace, have worked together throughout their married life to improve the quality of marriages—first in Britain, then in the United States, with further programs and projects throughout the world. David is a behavioral scientist with a Ph.D. from England, who has served as a professor in three American universities. Vera has an M.A. from Drew University in Madison, New Jersey, and has worked with her husband in many different countries to promote the cause of better marriages. In 1973 they established the Association for Couples in Marriage Enrichment (ACME), of which they were the first presidents. ACME has now become an international organization, with member couples currently in thirty-two different countries.

Here are some details about the contributors.

Alvis and Florence Carpenter took over the ACME program for newlyweds in Winston-Salem, North Carolina, after it had been started by Alice and Hampton Morgan. Alvis is an ordained minister in the Southern Baptist Convention with M.Div. and D.Min. degrees from the Southern Baptist Theological Seminary in Louisville, Kentucky. He is in the private practice of marriage and family counseling and is a clinical member of the American Association for Marriage and Family Therapy. Florence has an M.A. from Eastern Kentucky State University and taught music in public elementary school for twenty years. She is currently serving as coordinator of religious education for the Augsburg Lutheran Church in Winston-Salem.

Lyle and Terry Dykstra shared in the pioneering task of developing the newlywed program in Kansas City. They then moved to Baltimore, where they have developed a program for newlyweds, which was first organized by the Family and Children's Services agency and later taken over by a group of city churches. Lyle is a Presbyterian pastor with M.Div. and D.Min. degrees from Union Theological Seminary in New York and the McCormick Seminary in Chicago. Terry has a Master's degree in human development and family and community relations.

Linda and William McConahey live in South Boston, Virginia, and have established there a program for newlyweds, which is financed by the local community. Bill is a Harvard graduate and a physician, serving in a group practice. Linda is a psychologist with a Ph.D. They are not only members of the ACME organization, but also are currently its president couple.

Phyllis and Randy Michael were closely involved in the development of the newlyweds program in Kansas City, where they live. Phyllis has an M.A. in English language and literature and an M.S. in counseling and guidance. She has served as the director of the Marital Growth and Education in Marriage program for Family and Children's Services in Kansas City. Randy has a D.Min. degree in counseling and marriage enrichment and is now working for his Ph.D.

Alice and Richard Robertson both work at a training center for pastoral counselors in Columbus, Georgia. Alice is an inactive member of the Georgia Bar and currently is serving as director of community education for the Bradley Center, Inc., a nonprofit psychiatric hospital, which is the parent organization for the Pastoral Institute. Richard was one of the founders of the Pastoral Institute and is currently serving as its acting director. He is a United Methodist minister who has specialized in pastoral counseling and couple counseling. The Institute has now established a newlywed program entitled "Right Start."

Doris and Jerry Thompson played leading roles in the early development of the Kansas City newlyweds project. Jerry enlisted the support of a large number of local pastors, who persuaded the couples they married to sign up for the program. He is an ordained minister in the Christian Church (Disciples of Christ) with a Master's degree in religious education, an honorary D.D. from Phillips University Seminary, and has done post-graduate work in marriage and family life. Doris, a director of Christian education, has a B.S. in education and has done further study in marriage and family life. They have recently moved to Nashville, Tennessee.

APPENDIX 2

Some Other Books About Newlyweds

This book is by no means the first to be written about the early years of marriage. Here are ten other books you may be interested in knowing about. We have arranged them in the order of their dates of publication.

McGinnis, Tom. *Your First Year of Marriage.* New York: Doubleday, 1967. Written by a New Jersey marriage counselor, this was one of the early books in the field. It deals with communication, sex, family planning, in-laws, friends, and money. The foreword is by David Mace.

Small, Dwight Harvey. *After You've Said 'I Do.'* Old Tappan, N.J.: Fleming Revell, 1968. The focus is on effective communication in marriage. The author is a pastor, so the emphasis is on the early years of a Christian marriage.

Clinebell, Howard. *Growth Counseling for Marriage Enrichment: Pre-marriage and the Early Years.* Philadelphia: Fortress Press, 1975. This is an attempt by a qualified professional in the field to use marriage enrichment principles and practices to help couples start their marriages wisely and well.

Yancey, Phillip. *After the Wedding.* Waco, Texas: Word Books, 1976. The emphasis here is on the first five years of marriage. Nine different couples, in successive chapters, share their own early experiences of marriage, with comments from the author. Finally, there are comments from well-known authors Charlie Shedd and Paul Tournier and their wives.

WHEN THE HONEYMOON'S OVER

Garrett, Yvonne. *The Newlywed Handbook*. Waco, Texas: Word Books, 1981. Written by a Baptist woman after she had led a series of Sunday school classes for newlyweds, each class lasting for six months. Each chapter takes a different issue and begins with a series of questions that were used as "discussion starters." The class was confined to twelve couples.

Nilson, Jon. *From This Day Forward*. St. Meinrad, Ind.: Abbey Press, 1983. This is a small book of eighty-six pages, written by a professor at Loyola University. The subheading is "Challenges and Gifts of the Early Years of Marriage," and the approach is that of a Christian teacher.

Hart, Thomas and Hart, Kathleen. *The First Two Years of Marriage*. Mahwah, N.J.: Paulist Press, 1983. The authors are both teachers, writers, and counselors. This excellent book, with 132 pages, covers the ground very well, with exercises following each of ten chapters.

Drescher, John and Drescher, Betty. *If We Were Starting Our Marriage Again*. Nashville: Abingdon Press, 1985. Married more than thirty years, the authors look back and offer guidance to couples just starting. It is full of practical wisdom.

Piljac, Pamela. *Newlywed: A Survival Guide to the First Years of Marriage*. Portage, Ind.: Bryce-Waterton, 1985. With 253 pages, this book by the author of the *Bride-to-Bride Book* covers a wide field under four headings—Your Family, Your Home, Your Money, and Your Life.

Arond, Miriam and Pauker, Samuel. *The First Year of Marriage*. New York: Warner Books, 1987. This book is based on a major research. In 400 pages, we get the findings of personal contacts with 455 newlyweds, whose stories provide convincing evidence of the need to prepare couples more adequately for the difficult adjustments of modern marriage. This is a book to *study*, not just to read. The authors are a married couple, and Dr. Pauker is a psychiatrist.